First Language Lessons
for the Well-Trained Mind

Level 3

Student Workbook

by Jessie Wise and Sara Buffington

WELL-
TRAINED
MIND
PRESS

www.welltrainedmind.com

PHOTOCOPYING AND DISTRIBUTION POLICY

© 2007 Well-Trained Mind Press. Reprinted May 2024 by Mercury Print Productions

4 5 6 7 8 9 10 11 12 Mercury 29 28 27 26 25 24

FIRST LANGUAGE LESSONS, LEVEL 3

PAGE NUMBERS FOR LESSONS

Lesson 1.............. page 1	Lesson 24.......... page 73	Lesson 47........ page 149
Lesson 2.............. page 2	Lesson 25.......... page 78	Lesson 48........ page 152
Lesson 3 .... page 4	Lesson 26.......... page 80	Lesson 49........ page 154
Lesson 4.............. page 7	Lesson 27.......... page 84	Lesson 50........ page 156
Lesson 5............ page 11	Lesson 28.......... page 89	Lesson 51........ page 158
Lesson 6............ page 14	Lesson 29.......... page 92	Lesson 52........ page 160
Lesson 7............ page 17	Lesson 30.......... page 94	Lesson 53........ page 162
Lesson 8............ page 20	Lesson 31........ page 100	Lesson 54........ page 164
Lesson 9............ page 23	Lesson 32........ page 102	Lesson 55........ page 166
Lesson 10.......... page 25	Lesson 33........ page 108	Lesson 56........ page 171
Lesson 11 .... page 27	Lesson 34.........page 111	Lesson 57........ page 176
Lesson 12.......... page 29	Lesson 35........ page 117	Lesson 58........ page 182
Lesson 13.......... page 31	Lesson 36........ page 119	Lesson 59........ page 184
Lesson 14.......... page 34	Lesson 37........ page 121	Lesson 60........ page 188
Lesson 15.......... page 38	Lesson 38........ page 123	Lesson 61........ page 194
Lesson 16.......... page 43	Lesson 39........ page 127	Lesson 62........ page 199
Lesson 17.......... page 47	Lesson 40........ page 132	Lesson 63........ page 203
Lesson 18.......... page 50	Lesson 41........ page 135	Lesson 64........ page 205
Lesson 19.......... page 52	Lesson 42........ page 138	Lesson 65........ page 208
Lesson 20.......... page 57	Lesson 43........ page 142	Lesson 66........ page 209
Lesson 21.......... page 61	Lesson 44........ page 143	Lesson 67........ page 211
Lesson 22.......... page 65	Lesson 45........ page 145	Lesson 68........ page 215
Lesson 23.......... page 69	Lesson 46........ page 147	Lesson 69........ page 219

PAGE NUMBERS CONTINUE ON THE NEXT PAGE

LESSONS (CONTINUED)

Lesson 70 .... page 223

Lesson 71 .... page 226

Lesson 72 .... page 227

Lesson 73 .... page 231

Lesson 74 .... page 234

Lesson 75 .... page 237

Lesson 76 .... page 239

Lesson 77 .... page 241

Lesson 78 .... page 243

Lesson 79 .... page 247

Lesson 80 .... page 251

Lesson 81 .... page 257

Lesson 82 .... page 259

Lesson 83 .... page 263

Lesson 84 .... page 266

Lesson 85 .... page 268

Lesson 86 .... page 272

Lesson 87 .... page 275

Lesson 88 .... page 281

Lesson 89 .... page 286

Writing Letters Lesson 1 .... page 287

Writing Letters Lesson 2 .... page 289

Writing Letters Lesson 3 .... page 290

Writing Letters Lesson 4 .... page 293

Writing Letters Lesson 5 .... page 294

Writing Letters Lesson 6 .... page 297

Writing Letters Lesson 7 .... page 298

Dictionary Skills Lesson 1 .... page 299

Dictionary Skills Lesson 2 .... page 303

Dictionary Skills Lesson 3 .... page 305

Dictionary Skills Lesson 4 .... page 306

Dictionary Skills Lesson 5 .... page 308

Dictionary Skills Lesson 6 .... page 311

Dictionary Skills Lesson 7 .... page 314

Oral Usage Lesson 1 .... page 316

Oral Usage Lesson 2 .... page 317

Oral Usage Lesson 3 .... page 319

Oral Usage Lesson 4 .... page 321

Oral Usage Lesson 5 .... page 325

Oral Usage Lesson 6 .... page 329

Oral Usage Lesson 7 .... page 331

Definitions, Rules, and Lists ...... page 337

LESSON 1

Exercise 1

First Language Lessons

for the Well-Trained Mind

Level 3

Exercise 2

by Jessie Wise and Sara Buffington

Optional Dictation Exercise

LESSON 2

Exercise 1

hunger

excitement

sadness

Exercise 2

When I lost my favorite toy, I was filled with _____.

I trembled with _____ as I opened my biggest

birthday present.

My stomach made loud, rumbling noises because of

my _____.

Dictation Exercise

Nouns

LESSON 3

Exercise 1

Person	Place	Thing	Idea
child	room	pencil	love
mother	street	toy	anger

Exercise 2

firefighter

store

paper

peace

car

nurse

kindness

town

Person	Place	Thing	Idea

4

Exercise 3

● bee

bees

The other bees in the hive feed the queen bee.

cloud

clouds

One cloud was bigger and darker than the other clouds.

daughter

daughters

My mother has three daughters, and I am the youngest daughter.

● ## Exercise 4

A <u>hummingbird</u> is a very tiny bird.

Some <u>hummingbirds</u> build nests the size of walnuts and lay eggs the size of peas.

●

Exercise 5

The evening star is brighter than the other stars.

The oldest boy helped the younger boys.

That river joins two other rivers that flow to the sea.

A bird in the hand is worth two birds in the bush.

LESSON 4

New: Forming Plurals of Words That End in S, SH, CH, X, or Z

Review: Nouns

Review: Forming Plurals the Usual Way

Exercise 1

Person	Place	Thing	Idea
child	room	pencil	love
mother	street	toy	anger
firefighter	store	paper	peace
nurse	town	car	kindness

Exercise 2

button

park

honesty

playmate

Person	Place	Thing	Idea

Exercise 3

arm____

leg____

painter____

pond____

chair____

Exercise 4

s

sh

ch

x

z

Exercise 5

bus

buses

The empty bus arrived before the other buses.

bus____

dish

dishes

Do not drop a dish when you are washing the dishes.

dish____

8

inch

inches

Thirteen inches is the same as one foot plus one inch.

inch____

box

boxes

Wait until you have opened the other boxes before you open the big box.

box____

buzz

buzzes

In the game you may move one space when you hear one buzz and three spaces when you hear three buzzes.

buzz____

Exercise 6

1. My favorite glass is part of a set of colored glasses.

(Exercise 6 continues on the next page.)

2. A peach is a popular fruit in America, but peaches originally came from China.

3. Foxes have such good hearing that a red fox can hear a mouse squeak one hundred feet away.

4. Your brush probably has bristles made of nylon, but some brushes are made from the hair of pigs, camels, or squirrels.

LESSON 5

New: Forming Plurals of Nouns That End in Y

New: Irregular Plural Nouns

Review: Forming Plurals the Usual Way

Review: Forming Plurals of Words That End in S, SH, CH, X, or Z

Exercise 1

baby

babies

Exercise 2

Singular Noun	Change to a Plural Noun
penny	
lady	
sky	
fly	

Exercise 3

day

days

Exercise 4

Singular Noun	Change to a Plural Noun
boy	
key	
toy	
tray	

Exercise 5

Singular Noun	Irregular Plural Noun
child	children
foot	feet
tooth	teeth
man	men
woman	women
mouse	mice
goose	geese
deer	deer
fish	fish

Optional Dictation Exercise

LESSON 6

New: Common and Proper Nouns

Review: Forming Plurals

Exercise 1

Singular Noun	Change to a Plural Noun
book	
pan	
class	
watch	
city	
story	
monkey	
valley	
puppy	
sock	
turkey	
bush	

Exercise 2

1. I am a _____.

2. My name is _____.

3. Some proper names in my family are:

_____ [Instructor]

_____ [Student]

_____ [Instructor]

_____ [Student]

_____ [Instructor]

_____ [Student]

_____ [Instructor]

_____ [Student]

(Exercise 2 continues on the next page.)

15

Exercise 2 (continued)

4.   _____ [Instructor]

        I live in _____. [Student]

5.   My pet is a _____.

        The name of my pet is _____.

Optional Dictation Exercise

LESSON 7

New: Pronouns

Review: Common and Proper Nouns

Exercise 1

Pronouns

I, me, my, mine

You, your, yours

He, she, him, her, it

His, hers, its

We, us, our, ours

They, them, their, theirs

Exercise 2

1. George Washington was the first president of the United States. _____

2. The Roman Empire was divided into two parts. _____

3. Mother read the tale called *The Adventures of Spider* to my sister and me. _____

4. The Battle of Hastings was an important event in England's history. _____

5. April showers bring May flowers. The child gave the flowers to her friend. _____

6. Empress Theodora was the wife of Justinian, who ruled the Byzantine Empire. _____

(Exercise 2 continues on the next page.)

Exercise 2 (continued)

7. That game is <u>Carla's and mine</u>. _____

8. <u>The Smith family's</u> car is blue. _____

9. One of <u>Galileo's</u> discoveries was that the moon shone by reflecting the light of the sun. _____

10. <u>You and I</u> are able to cool ourselves by sweating and warm ourselves by exercising. _____

11. One reason that the first Queen Elizabeth did not marry is that she wanted decisions to be solely <u>Queen Elizabeth's</u>. _____

12. *Pinocchio*, a book written by <u>Carlo Collodi</u>, teaches us that lying is wrong. _____

13. <u>King Ferdinand and Queen Isabella</u> gave Columbus ships and sup-plies for his journey across the seas. _____

14. My older brother read <u>my sister's and my</u> copy of *Pilgrim's Progress* to Jane. _____

15. No two people have the same fingerprints. Mine are different from <u>my sister's and brother's</u>. _____

(Choose from these pronouns to fill in the blanks)
I, me, my, mine
You, your, yours
He, she, him, her, it
His, hers, its
We, us, our, ours
They, them, their, theirs

Dictation Exercise

LESSON 8

Exercise 1

fork

_____

Exercise 2

glass

_____

dish

_____

inch

_____

box

_____

buzz

_____

Exercise 3

story

_____

Exercise 4

toy

_____

Exercise 5

Pronouns

I, me, my, mine

You, your, yours

He, she, him, her, it

His, hers, its

We, us, our, ours

They, them, their, theirs

How Animals Use Their Tails

Many animals have tails, and (1) animals use their tails in different ways. The squirrel uses (2) the squirrel's tail to help it balance in the treetops. Crocodiles use their spiked tails to help (3) crocodiles swim through the water. (4) Crocodiles' tails also help them to knock small animals into water where they can be easily captured. A mother rabbit's tiny white tail guides (5) the mother rabbit's babies, or kits, through bushes and tall grasses. (6) The mother rabbit will lead her kits back to the safety of the burrow. The male peacock uses (7) the male peacock's tail feathers to attract a female. (8) The male peacock will spread his colorful feathers and parade in front of a female peacock. The beaver has a flat tail. (9) The beaver uses its tail to pat down mud to make its home.

Optional Dictation Exercise

LESSON 9

The Land of Nod
by Robert Louis Stevenson

From breakfast on through all the day
At home among my friends I stay;
But every night I go abroad
Afar into the land of Nod.

All by myself I have to go,
With none to tell me what to do—
All alone beside the streams
And up the mountainsides of dreams.

The strangest things are there for me,
Both things to eat and things to see,
And many frightening sights abroad
Till morning in the land of Nod.

Try as I like to find the way,
I never can get back by day,
Nor can remember plain and clear
The curious music that I hear.

(This lesson continues on the next page.)

☐ My instructor read the title, the author, and the poem to me. We talked about its meaning.

Next we read the poem three times during the lesson.

☐ one

☐ two

☐ three

Later in the day we read the poem three times.

☐ one

☐ two

☐ three

And then we read the poem three more times.

☐ one

☐ two

☐ three

Optional Dictation Exercise

LESSON 10

New: Action Verbs

Exercise 1

Active Animals
Anonymous

The monkey swings.
The robin sings.

The cow moos.
The dove coos.

The cat stretches.
The dog fetches.

The camel walks.
The tiger stalks.

The mouse scurries.
The ant hurries.

The bear growls.
The wolf howls.

The lion roars.
The eagle soars.

Exercise 2

1.   The worm wriggles in the dirt.

2.   The parents laugh at the child's joke.

3.   I snuggle next to my mom.

4.   My sister sneezed.

5.   My rabbit nibbles his food.

6.   The bird flew over the house.

7.   The squirrel climbs up a tree.

8.   The deer runs through the woods.

Verbs
by Eleanor Farjeon

Nouns are things I see and touch,

My **cake**, my **mother**, and my **ball**;

I like some nouns very much,

Though some I do not like at all.

Verbs are the things I do, and make,

And feel, in one way or another.

Thanks to verbs, I *eat* my cake,

And *throw* my ball, and *hug* my mother.

Yet verbs, which make me laugh and play,

Can also make me cry and fall,

And *tease* my mother every day,

And *spoil* my cake, and *lose* my ball!

Dictation Exercise

LESSON 11

New: Definition of a Sentence

New: Sentences (Diagramming Subjects and Action Verbs)

Exercise 1

Emily sings.

Bubbles float.

Dogs bark.

Exercise 2

Exercise 3

Bubbles float.

Exercise 4

1. Birds fly.

    —————————|—————————

2. Children run.

    —————————|—————————

3. He giggles.

    —————————|—————————

Optional Dictation Exercise

LESSON 12

Bats

Bats are very strange little animals, having hair like mice, and wings like birds. During the day, they live in cracks of rocks, in caves, and in other dark places.

At night, they go forth in search of food; and no doubt, you have seen them flying about, catching such insects as happen to be out rather late at night.

The wings of a bat have no feathers. They are only thin pieces of skin stretched upon a framework of bones. Besides this, it may be said that while he is a quadruped, he can rise into the air and fly from place to place like a bird.

(This lesson continues on the next page.)

LESSON 13

Exercise 1

Nathan yelled.

Exercise 2

She looked.

Exercise 3

brown dog

chubby dog

short dog

friendly dog

wet dog

playful dog

Exercise 4

Adjectives tell
- what kind
- which one
- how many
- whose

Exercise 5

this dog

that dog

these dogs

those dogs

Exercise 6

first dog

second dog

next dog

last dog

Exercise 7

one dog

two dogs

forty-three dogs

Exercise 8

many dogs

several dogs

all dogs

both dogs

some dogs

another dog

each dog

more dogs

most dogs

other dogs

Dictation Exercise

LESSON 14

Exercise 1

purple

yellow

sweet

stinky

soft

smooth

prickly

velvety

huge

tiny

Exercise 2

this flower

that flower

these flowers

those flowers

34

Exercise 3

first flower

second flower

next flower

last flower

Exercise 4

1. **Three** cats mewed.

2. **Twenty** worms squirmed.

3. **All** people blink.

4. **Both** clowns juggled.

Exercise 5

This shirt belongs to the boy.

It is the **boy's** shirt.

Exercise 6

the **librarian's** desk

the **painter's** brush

the **farmer's** tractor

the **player's** trophy

the **lion's** roar

Aunt Glinda's pie

Mother's dinner

Taylor's guitar

Jennifer's ticket

Exercise 7

Noun	Adjective That Tells Whose
man	the _____ head
bird	the _____ nest
child	the _____ toy
Juan	_____ shoes
Uncle Abram	_____ car

Exercise 8

These shirts belong to the boys.

These are the **boys'** shirts.

Exercise 9

two **friends'** lollipops

several **kittens'** mews

many **singers'** voices

the **actors'** costumes

the **Parkers'** cars

Exercise 10

Noun	Adjective That Tells Whose
shoppers	the _____ baskets
girls	the _____ dresses
Richards	the _____ children
trees	the _____ leaves

1. The shoppers' baskets are here.

2. The painter's brush dripped.

Exercise 11

1. The actors' costumes are in that room.

2. Mother's dinner was ham and potatoes.

3. The trees' leaves droop.

LESSON 15

Exercise 1

this shirt

that shirt

these shirts

those shirts

Exercise 2

first flower

eighth flower

next flower

final flower

Exercise 3

● **several** cars

all cars

both cars

some cars

another car

each car

more cars

most cars

other cars

Exercise 4

● It is the **boy's** shirt.

Exercise 5

Noun	Adjective That Tells Whose
cat	the _____ fur
book	the _____ cover
Lee	_____ coat

Exercise 6

The **girls'** dresses are all white.

●

Exercise 7

Noun	Adjective That Tells Whose
foxes	the _____ dens
flowers	the _____ seeds
Wilders	the _____ pets

Exercise 8

Singular Noun	Plural Noun
child	children
foot	feet
tooth	teeth
man	men
woman	women
mouse	mice
goose	geese
deer	deer
sheep	sheep
fish	fish

Exercise 9

two **deer's** antlers

many **fish's** scales

several **mice's** nests

Exercise 10

Noun	Adjective That Tells Whose
children	the _____ games
men	the _____ ties
sheep	the _____ pens

Exercise 11

Singular Noun	Plural Noun
kitten	kittens

Singular Noun	Plural Noun
glass	glasses
brush	brushes
peach	peaches
box	boxes
buzz	buzzes

Singular Noun	Plural Noun
family	families

Singular Noun	Plural Noun
day	days

LESSON 16

Exercise 1

sweet

crumbly

chocolate

strawberry

white

thick

gooey

delicious

birthday

Exercise 2

1.   Two people laughed.

2.   Sixty geese flew.

3.   All windows close.

4.   Both feet itch.

5.   Some plants froze.

6.   Another child yells.

(Exercise 2 continues on the next page.)

Exercise 2 (continued)

7. Each flower opens.

8. More rain falls.

9. Most birds hop.

10. Other birds waddle.

Exercise 3

Noun	Adjective That Tells Whose
cricket	the _____ body
turkeys	the _____ necks
women	the _____ class

Exercise 4

Articles

Articles are little words,

You need know only three.

The articles that describe nouns

are **a**, **an**, **the**.

An automobile speeds.

The kettle whistles.

A truck rattles.

The snake slithers.

A camel spits.

An owl hoots.

Exercise 5

Cats purr.

Fat cats purr.

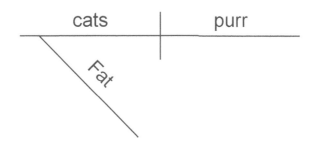

Exercise 6

1. Hot cocoa steams.

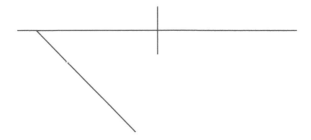

2. Three friends shop.

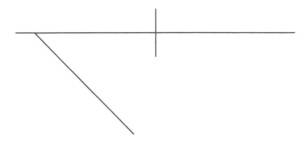

(Exercise 6 continues on the next page.)

Exercise 6 (continued)

3.   Most gold shines.

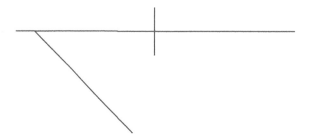

4.   Children's bikes zip.

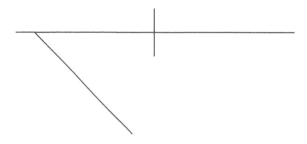

5.   The alarm rang.

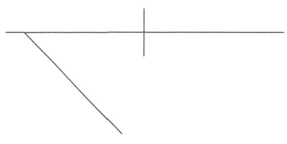

Optional Follow-Up

engine

potato

insect

leaf

umbrella

onion

car

LESSON 17

Exercise 1

Tall trees sway.

That door squeaks.

Several cars race.

Mandy's horse neighs.

Exercise 2

An engine roared.

The soup boiled.

A team cheered.

Exercise 3

Cats purr.

Fat cats purr.

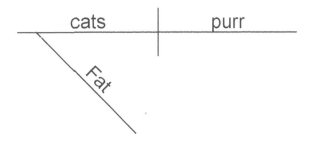

(Exercise 3 continues on the next page.)

Exercise 3 (continued)

Furry, fat cats purr.

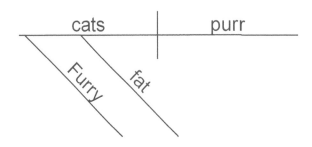

Exercise 4

1. Ten white swans swim.

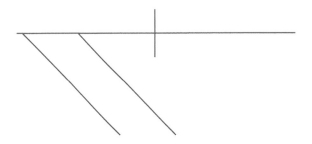

2. The musicians' trumpets sound.

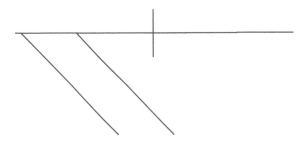

3. Many cheerful robins chirp.

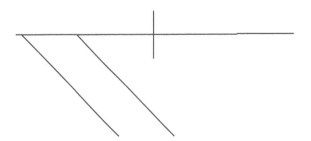

4.   Snakes' beady eyes shine.

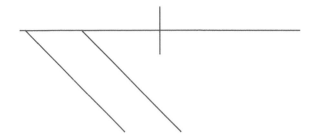

Optional Follow-Up

- a tall, green tree

- ten tiny, blue flowers

- a fat, lazy cat

- a huge yellow house

- first dog; next dog; last dog

- some birds; more birds; many birds

LESSON 18

A Tragic Story

by William Makepeace Thackeray

There lived a sage in days of yore,
And he a handsome pigtail wore;
But wondered much and sorrowed more,
Because it hung behind him.

He mused upon the curious case,
And swore he'd change the pigtail's place,
And have it hanging at his face,
Not dangling there behind him.

Says he, "The mystery I've found—
I'll turn me round"—he turned him round;
But still it hung behind him.

Then round and round, and out and in,
All day the puzzled sage did spin;
In vain—it mattered not a pin—
The pigtail hung behind him.

And right and left, and round about,
And up and down, and in and out,
He turned; but still the pigtail stout
Hung steadily behind him.

And though his efforts never slack,
And though he twist, and twirl, and tack,
Alas! still faithful to his back,
The pigtail hangs behind him.

☐ My instructor read the title, the author, and the poem to me. We talked about its meaning.

Next we read the poem three times during the lesson.
☐ one
☐ two
☐ three

Later in the day we read the poem three times.
☐ one
☐ two
☐ three

And then we read the poem three more times.
☐ one
☐ two
☐ three

Dictation Exercise

LESSON 19

Exercise 1

Adverbs tell

- how
- when
- where
- how often
- to what extent

Exercise 2

I laugh **quietly**.

I laugh **happily**.

I laugh **quickly**.

I laugh **nervously**.

I laugh **loudly**.

Exercise 3

quickly

quietly

slowly

I eat _____.

loudly

sweetly

merrily

I sing _____.

carefully

clearly

neatly

I write _____.

shyly

broadly

warmly

I smile _____.

joyously

busily

rambunctiously

I play _____.

Exercise 4

Cats purr.

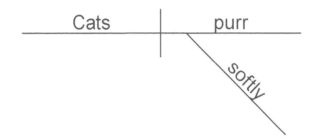

Cats purr softly.

Waterfalls tumble.

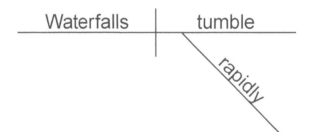

Waterfalls tumble rapidly.

1.   Ants work busily.

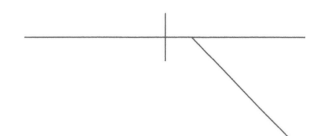

2.   Clouds float silently.

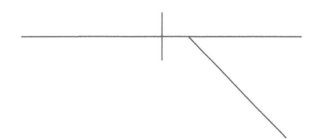

3.   Bears sleep deeply.

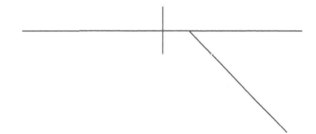

4.   Pigs snort noisily.

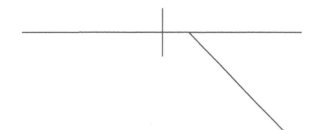

Optional Follow-Up

Subject	Verb	Adverb
Knights	battle	fiercely
Turtles	lumber	cautiously
Spies	wink	mysteriously
Dancers	leap	gracefully
Eagles	cry	shrilly
Babies	toddle	awkwardly

New: Adverbs That Tell When (with Diagramming)

Exercise 1

Adverbs tell
- how
- when
- where
- how often
- to what extent

Exercise 2

I leave **tonight**.

I leave **tomorrow**.

I leave **soon**.

I leave **now**.

I leave **immediately**.

Exercise 3

early

now

late

I eat _____.

(Exercise 3 continues on the next page.)

yesterday

earlier

already

I sang _____.

today

again

promptly

I wrote _____.

then

lately

before

I smiled _____.

momentarily

later

tonight

I play _____.

Exercise 4

Taylor whistled.

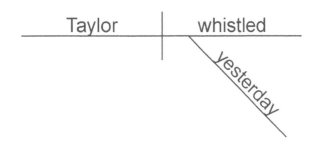

Taylor whistled yesterday.

She arrived.

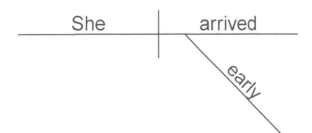

She arrived early.

Exercise 5

1. Lee sneezed already.

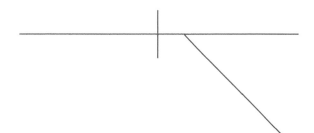

2. Mom shopped yesterday.

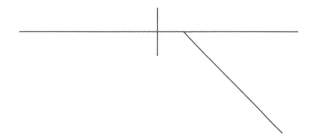

3. Lizards laze today.

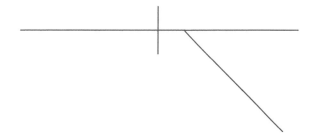

4. I yawn now.

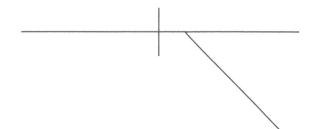

LESSON 21

New: Adverbs That Tell Where (with Diagramming)

Exercise 1

I run **nearby**.

I run **outside**.

I run **upstairs**.

I run **away**.

I run **far**.

Exercise 2

here

inside

downstairs

I eat _____.

everywhere

outside

nearby

I sing _____.

outdoors

anywhere

upstairs

I play _____.

Exercise 2 (continued)

away

far

forward

I walk _____.

Exercise 3

Hummingbirds fly.

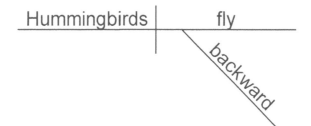

Hummingbirds fly backward.

Columbus traveled.

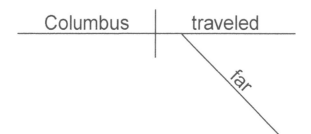

Columbus traveled far.

Exercise 4

1. Bubbles drift upward.

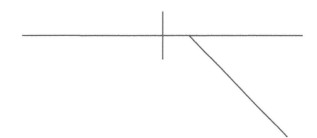

2. I searched everywhere.

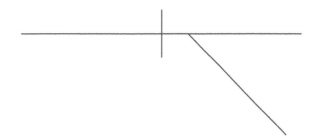

3. Children play outside.

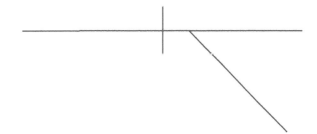

4. Abby came here.

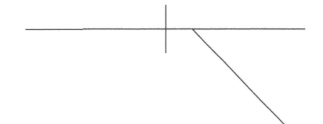

Optional Follow-Up

I walk **nearby**.

I walk **backward**.

I walk **upstairs**.

I walk **away**.

I walk **far**.

I walk **sideways**.

LESSON 22

Exercise 1

I exercise **daily**.

I exercise **hourly**.

I exercise **rarely**.

I exercise **usually**.

I exercise **frequently**.

Exercise 2

sometimes

nightly

hourly

I read _____.

seldom

often

daily

I nap _____.

regularly

rarely

weekly

I share _____.

Exercise 2 (continued)

once

frequently

daily

I complained _____.

Exercise 3

You breathe.

You breathe constantly.

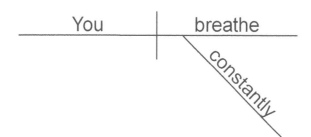

Logan tripped.

Logan tripped twice.

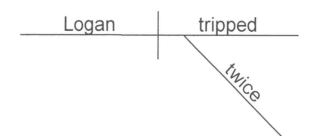

Exercise 4

1. Owls hunt nightly.

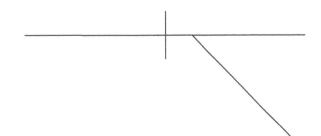

2. Musicians tune often.

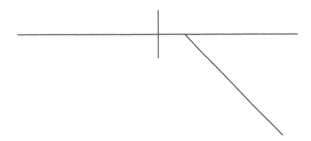

3. I relax sometimes.

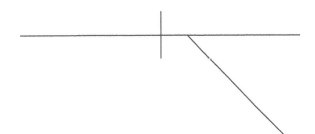

4. Kayla studies daily.

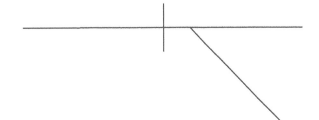

Exercise 5

I **always** think.

She **never** quarrels.

Tom **seldom** drives.

LESSON 23

Exercise 1

Fresh buds open.

That insect bites.

Six teams travel.

Chip's foot twitches.

Exercise 2

A sword clanked.

The potato exploded.

An anteater snuffled.

Exercise 3

Green worms inch.

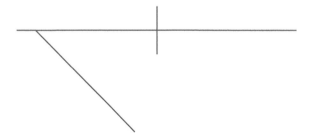

Exercise 4

I speak **clearly**.

I speak **rapidly**.

I speak **quietly**.

I speak **slowly**.

I speak **plainly**.

Exercise 5

quickly

quietly

loudly

sweetly

I sneeze _____.

Exercise 6

I spoke **earlier**.

I spoke **today**.

I spoke **yesterday**.

I spoke **afterward**.

I spoke **promptly**.

Exercise 7

yesterday

earlier

today

I hiccupped _____.

Exercise 8

I tiptoe **here**.

I tiptoe **there**.

I tiptoe **forward**.

I tiptoe **inside**.

I tiptoe **upstairs**.

Exercise 9

●

    downstairs

    outside

    nearby

    I cook _____.

Exercise 10

    I bathe **daily**.

    I bathe **yearly**.

    I bathe **often**.

    I **always** bathe.

    I **never** bathe.

Exercise 11

●

    yearly

    rarely

    frequently

    I travel _____.

Exercise 12

    Worms inch forward.

●

Exercise 13

Green worms inch forward.

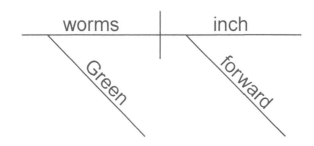

Exercise 14

1. Each horse gallops easily.

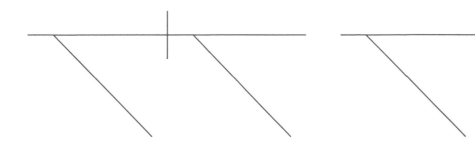

2. Strong winds blew again.

3. The alarm rang downstairs.

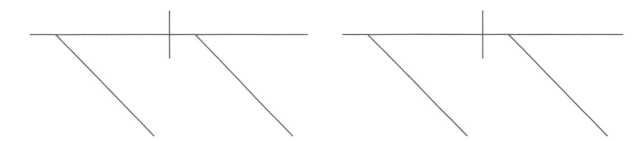

4. Lazy lizards lounge often.

LESSON 24

Exercise 1

Singular Noun	Change to a Plural Noun
kitten	
street	

Exercise 2

Singular Noun	Change to a Plural Noun
glass	
brush	
peach	
box	
buzz	

Exercise 3

Singular Noun	Change to a Plural Noun
family	
lady	

Exercise 4

Singular Noun	Change to a Plural Noun
day	
key	

Exercise 5

Pronouns

I, me, my, mine

You, your, yours

He, she, him, her, it

His, hers, its

We, us, our, ours

They, them, their, theirs

Exercise 6

Nancy gave grape juice to <u>me</u>.

I will ask <u>you</u> for permission.

Return <u>it</u> to the library.

The family will take <u>her</u> to the zoo.

Exercise 7

- sing
- run
- dance
- skip
- squat
- bend
- laugh
- sit

Exercise 8

- loud
- new
- tall
- beautiful
- silver
- warm

Exercise 9

- this
- these
- those
- first
- second
- next
- last

Exercise 10

- one
- ten
- seventy
- many
- each
- another
- all

Exercise 11

- **Jenny's**
- the **man's**
- the **dog's**
- all the **cats'**
- several **cooks'**
- the **children's**
- the **women's**

I jump quickly.

How	When	Where	How Often
happily	tonight	around	hourly
loudly	today	down	daily
quickly	now	far	nightly
quietly	again	inside	sometimes
sadly	immediately	nearby	rarely
softly	afterward	up	often
fast	momentarily	there	regularly

How do I jump?

I jump _____.

I jump _____.

When do I jump?

I jump _____.

I jump _____.

Where do I jump?

I jump _____.

I jump _____.

How often do I jump?

I jump _____.

I jump _____.

Exercise 13

quietly

today

rarely

nearby

happily

sometimes

again

inside

The Mongols

The Mongols came from the wild, cold mountains north of China. They lived in felt tents which they took down each morning, leaving nothing but ashes behind. They were nomads who swept over the countryside, conquering and killing. The bone-chilling cold of the north didn't stop them; they wore furs and leather and rubbed their skin with grease to keep the wind away. They never settled down and grew crops; instead they ate foxes, rabbits, and other small wild creatures. But they could go without food for days at a time. If they were in danger of starving, they would open the veins of their horses, drink some blood, and then close the vein and ride on.

New: Proper Nouns (with Diagramming)

Exercise 1

George Washington Carver

_____ [Instructor]

_____ [Student]

_____ [Instructor]

_____ [Student]

Exercise 2

George Washington Carver farmed.

George Washington Carver	farmed

Exercise 3

1. Thomas Alva Edison invented.

_____ | _____

2. Marian Anderson sang.

_____ | _____

Exercise 4

Yellowstone National Park

Central Park

Chobe National Park

Empire State Building

Sistine Chapel

Exercise 5

Months of the Year
January
February
March
April
May
June
July
August
September
October
November
December

Days of the Week
Monday
Tuesday
Wednesday
Thursday
Friday
Saturday
Sunday

My birthday is in _____.

Today is _____.

Exercise 6

Seasons
spring
summer
fall
winter

Optional Dictation Exercise

New: Helping Verbs (with Diagramming)

Exercise 1

point

stretch

wink

smile

hop

sigh

fall

roar

crawl

Exercise 2

Helping Verbs

am

is

are, was, were

be

being

been

have, has, had

do, does, did

shall, will, should, would, may, might, must

can, could

Exercise 3

Today you **play**.

Yesterday you **did play**.

Tomorrow you **will play**.

Exercise 4

1. Mr. Park **was painting** his house last year.

2. I **will bake** a cake tomorrow.

3. Yesterday, the baby **crawled** for the first time.

4. I **open** the door.

5. You **shall help** me next week.

6. He **smiles** at the joke.

Exercise 5

I am singing.

Exercise 6

1. They have eaten.

2. Mice will nibble.

3. We should watch.

_____|_____
                 |

4. Lucy had finished.

_____|_____
                 |

Optional Follow-Up

Mr. Park **was painting** his house last year.

I **will bake** a cake tomorrow.

Yesterday, the baby **did crawl** for the first time.

Victor **plays** the piano.

I **open** the door.

You **shall help** me next week.

Sandra **did kick** the ball.

He **smiles** at the joke.

TIME GAUGE

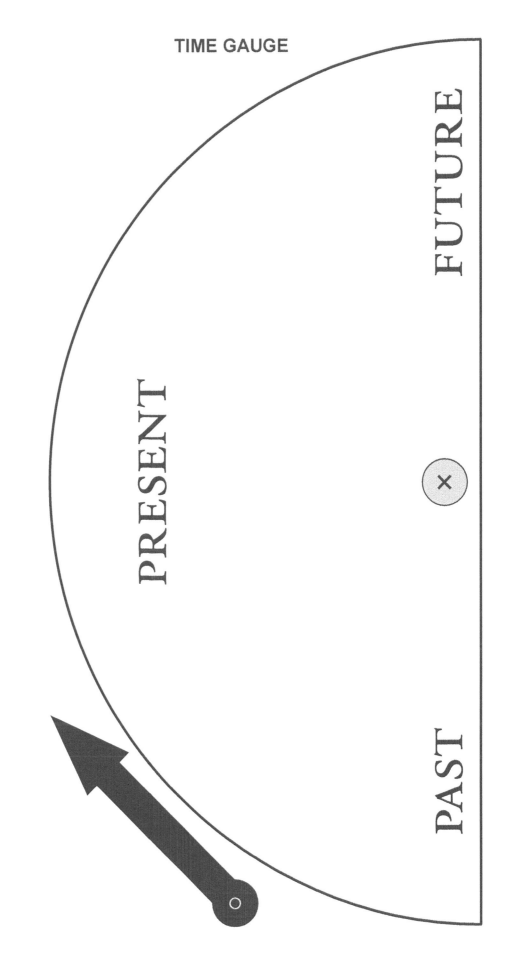

LESSON 28

Exercise 1

Seasons
spring
summer
fall
winter

Exercise 2

Months of the Year	Days of the Week
January	Monday
February	Tuesday
March	Wednesday
April	Thursday
May	Friday
June	Saturday
July	Sunday
August	
September	
October	
November	
December	

Exercise 3

Ferdinand Magellan

Exercise 4

Ferdinand Magellan sailed.

Ferdinand Magellan	sailed

Exercise 5

Louisa May Alcott wrote.

Exercise 6

We are chanting.

We	are chanting

Exercise 7

1. Bill Gates has donated.

_____ | _____

2. Pope Benedict XVI is praying.

_____ | _____

3. George Washington was fighting.

_____ | _____

4. Winston Churchill was speaking.

_____ | _____

LESSON 29

Exercise 1

Leroy kicks.

Exercise 2

Leroy kicks rocks.

Exercise 3

Ted cracked peanuts.

Mary kissed Mother.

Bethany scrubbed dishes.

We invited guests.

Exercise 4

Leroy kicks rocks.

Leroy	kicks	rocks

Exercise 5

1. Ted cracked peanuts.

2. Mary kissed Mother.

3. Bethany scrubbed dishes.

4. We invited guests.

Optional Dictation Exercise

Jane Addams started a program in 1889 to help people who had come to live in America from other countries. Newcomers came to live at a mansion called Hull House where they could study, learn crafts and skills, and live in a safe, healthy place. Although Jane Addams helped all kinds of people, she particularly cared for children and women.

LESSON 30

Exercise 1

John stirs soup.

Helpful John stirs soup.

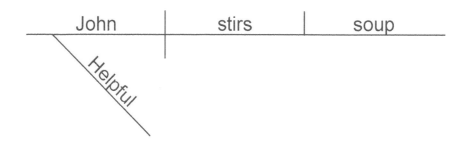

Helpful John stirs hot soup.

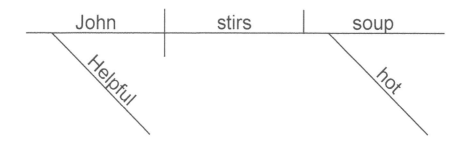

Helpful John stirs hot soup slowly.

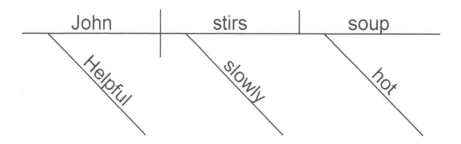

94

Exercise 2

● Spiders spin webs.

Most spiders spin webs.

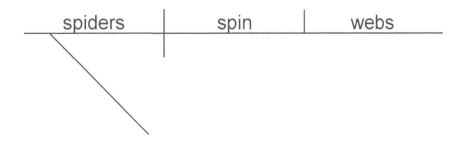

Most spiders spin sticky webs.

●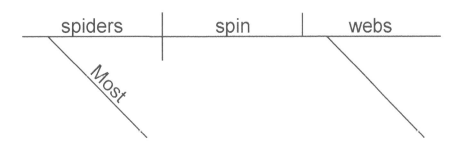

Most spiders spin sticky webs beautifully.

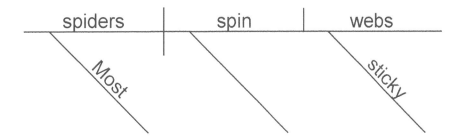

●

Exercise 3

Trish eats squid.

Bold Trish eats squid.

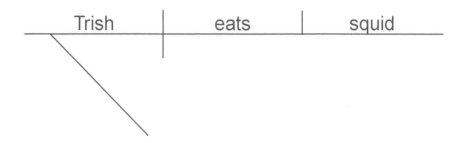

Bold Trish eats fried squid.

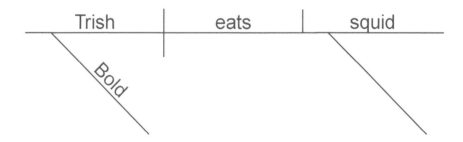

Bold Trish eats fried squid downstairs.

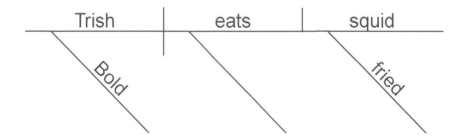

Exercise 4

Mothers rock babies.

Many mothers rock babies.

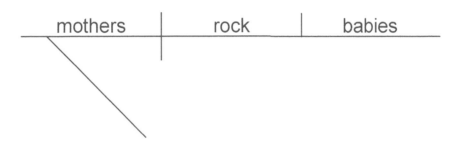

Many mothers rock tiny babies.

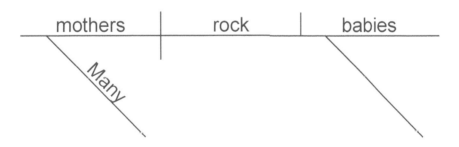

Many mothers rock tiny babies daily.

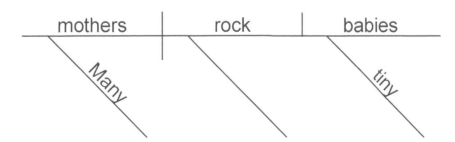

Optional Follow-Up

Ostriches lay eggs.

Tall ostriches lay eggs.

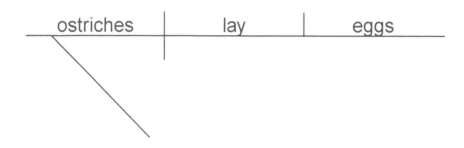

Tall ostriches lay enormous eggs.

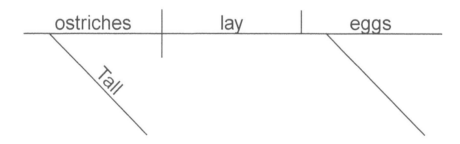

Tall ostriches lay enormous eggs here.

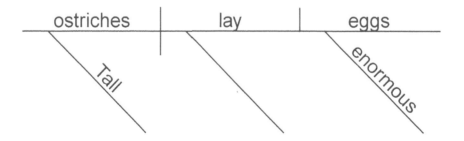

Optional Follow-Up (continued)

● Lions chase ostriches.

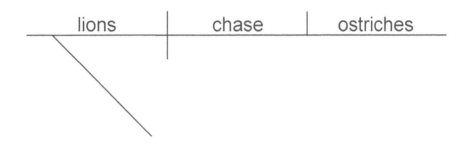

Fearsome lions chase ostriches.

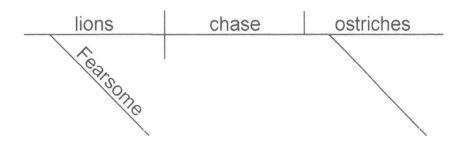

Fearsome lions chase speedy ostriches.

●

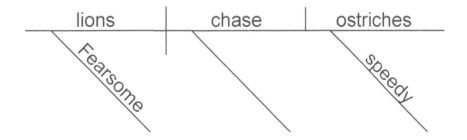

Fearsome lions chase speedy ostriches sometimes.

●

I Wandered Lonely As a Cloud

by William Wordsworth

I wandered Lonely As a Cloud
That floats on high o'er vales and hills,
When all at once I saw a crowd,
A host, of golden daffodils;

Beside the lake, beneath the trees,
Fluttering and dancing in the breeze.
Continuous as the stars that shine
And twinkle in the milky way,

They stretched in never-ending line
Along the margin of the bay;
Ten thousand saw I at a glance,
Tossing their heads in sprightly dance.

☐ My instructor read the title, the author, and the poem to me. We talked about its meaning.

Next we read the poem three times during the lesson.

☐ one

☐ two

☐ three

Later in the day we read the poem three times.

☐ one

☐ two

☐ three

And then we read the poem three more times.

☐ one

☐ two

☐ three

<u>Optional Dictation Exercise</u>

LESSON 32

Exercise 1

Hot chocolate warms cold children quickly.

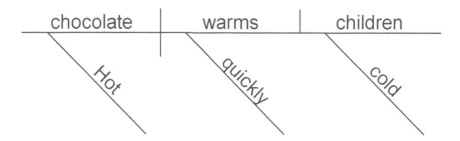

Exercise 2

Most spiders spin sticky webs beautifully.

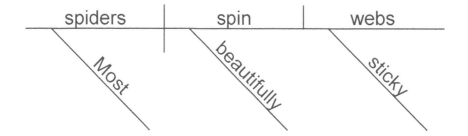

Exercise 3

Tornadoes uproot trees.

Twisty tornadoes uproot trees.

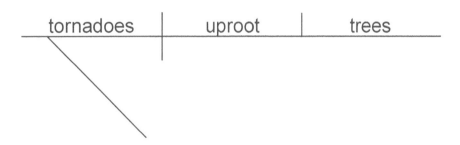

Twisty tornadoes uproot giant trees.

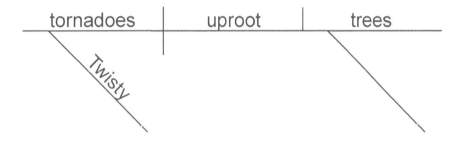

Twisty tornadoes uproot giant trees easily.

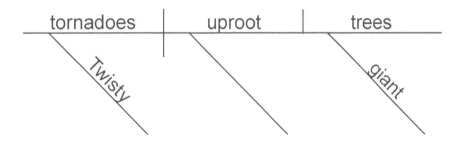

Exercise 4

Hail pounds crops.

Icy hail pounds crops.

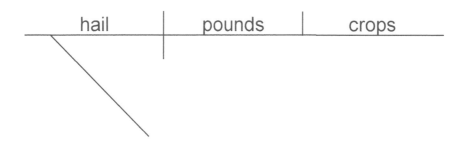

Icy hail pounds valuable crops.

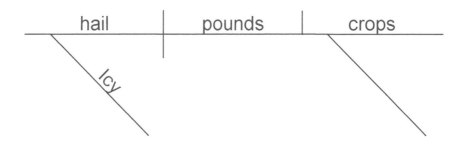

Icy hail pounds valuable crops yearly.

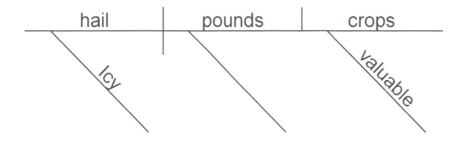

Exercise 5

Rains flooded rivers.

Heavy rains flooded rivers.

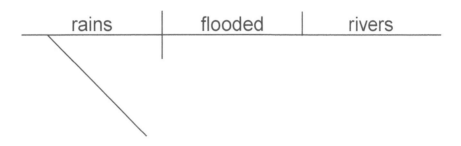

Heavy rains flooded several rivers.

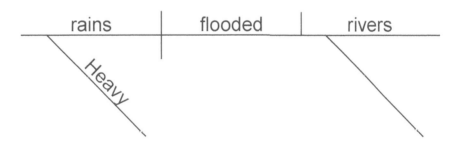

Heavy rains flooded several rivers nearby.

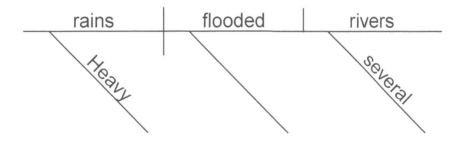

Optional Follow-Up

Tractors push dirt.

Huge tractors push dirt.

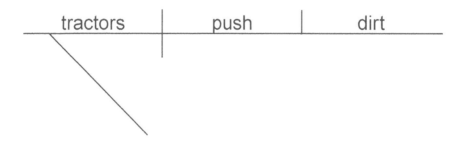

Huge tractors push heavy dirt.

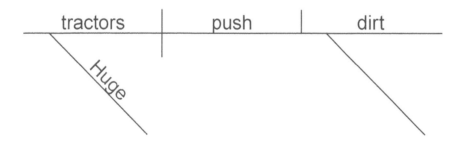

Huge tractors push heavy dirt steadily.

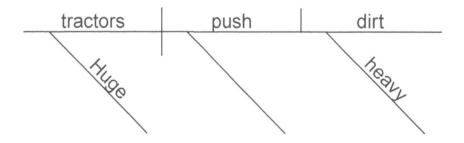

Optional Follow-Up (continued)

Cranes shift beams.

Giant cranes shift beams.

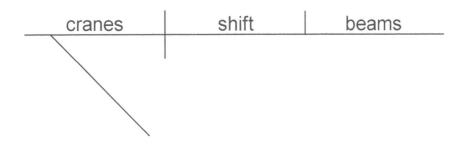

Giant cranes shift long beams.

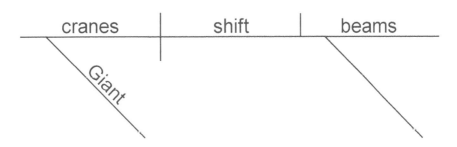

Giant cranes shift long beams sideways.

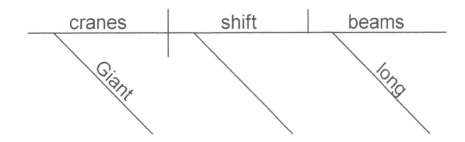

LESSON 33

Exercise 1

1. The boat floats.

2. She drank lemonade.

3. The eagle soared above.

Exercise 2

Squirrels are leaping.

Squirrels	are leaping

Exercise 3

Are you in the car?

I **am**.

Is your brother in the car with you?

He **is**.

Is your mother in the car with you?

She **is**.

Is your book on the seat?

It **is**.

108

Exercise 3 (continued)

●
    Who is in the car?

    We **are**.

    Who is beside you?

    You **are**.

    Who is outside the car?

    They **are**.

    Who was at the library yesterday?

    You **were**.

    Who else was at the library?

    She **was**.

Exercise 4

●
    Will you be at the campsite?

    I will **be**.

    Will Tim be at the campsite, too?

    He might **be**.

    Who has been there before?

    They have **been**.

●

Exercise 5

It is.

They are.

You were.

Dictation Exercise

LESSON 34

New: Linking Verbs (with Diagramming)

New: Predicate Nominatives (with Diagramming)

Review: Action Verbs, Helping Verbs, and State of Being Verbs

Exercise 1

1. An artist paints pictures.

2. Engineers design skyscrapers.

3. Composers write music.

Exercise 2

The chicken may squawk.

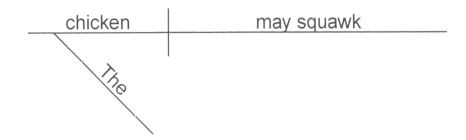

Exercise 3

Are you still in bed?

I **am**.

Is your sister still in the room, too?

She **is**.

(Exercise 3 continues on the next page.)

111

Was she in bed?

She **was**.

Is your breakfast on the table?

It **is**.

Who is at the bottom of the stairs?

You **are**.

Who is upstairs?

We **are**.

Is your father in the kitchen?

He **is**.

Are the twins at the table already?

They **are**.

Who was just in the kitchen with the rest of the family?

You **were**.

Is French toast on the breakfast table?

It **is**.

Are you still in bed?

Now I **am** not!

Exercise 4

Will you be in the yard?

I will **be**.

Should Tim be in the yard, too?

He should **be**.

Who has been in the yard this morning?

She has **been**.

Exercise 5

The verbs *am, is, are, was, were, be, being, been* can

- help another verb
- show a state of being
- link two words together

Exercise 6

Honeybees **are** insects.

Exercise 7

I **am** Sara.

Exercise 8

They **were** firefighters.

Exercise 9

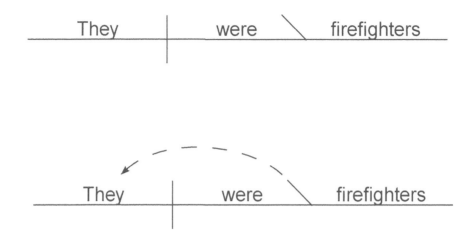

Exercise 10

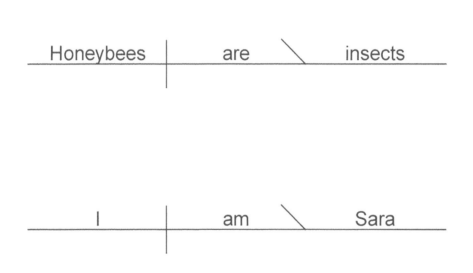

114

Exercise 11

Juncos are snowbirds.

Juncos	are \ snowbirds

Exercise 12

Kim baked a cookie.

Kim is a girl.

Exercise 13

Kim baked a _____.

Kim is a _____.

Dictation Exercise

Optional Follow-Up

I am _____.

My mother is _____.

My father is _____.

My sister is _____.

My cousin is _____.

My grandfather is _____.

LESSON 35

Exercise 1

Boy Scouts **are** volunteers.

Boy Scouts | are \ volunteers

Exercise 2

1. She is Carrie.

2. Yesterday was Tuesday.

3. Indians were hunters.

4. Settlers were farmers.

117

Optional Follow-Up

1. Wombats are _____.

   a. marsupials

   b. amphibians

   c. birds

2. Pangolins are _____.

   a. lizards

   b. plants

   c. anteaters

3. The duck-billed platypus is a _____.

   a. bird

   b. mammal

   c. creature from outer space

The Beaver Is a Builder

Beavers build themselves most curious huts to live in, and quite frequently a great number of these huts are placed close together, like the buildings in a town. They always build their huts on the banks of rivers or lakes, for they swim much more easily than they walk, and prefer moving about in the water.

When they build on the bank of a running stream, they make a dam across the stream for the purpose of keeping the water at the height they want. These dams are chiefly of mud and stones, and the branches of trees. They are sometimes six or seven hundred feet in length.

Their huts are made of the same materials as the dams, and are round in shape. The walls are very thick, and the roofs are finished off with a thick layer of mud. They commence building their houses in the summer, but do not get them finished before the early frosts. The freezing makes them tighter and stronger.

LESSON 37

New: Predicate Adjectives (with Diagramming)

Review: Linking Verbs

Review: Predicate Nominatives

Exercise 1

It was she.

Exercise 2

Snakes are reptiles.

Exercise 3

The sky **is** _____.

Pencils **are** _____.

The fried chicken **was** _____.

Exercise 4

Mountains are enormous.

Exercise 5

1. Kittens are cute.

2. I am kind.

3. John is tall.

4. They were clean.

LESSON 38

Review: Linking Verbs

Review: Predicate Adjectives

Review: Predicate Nominatives

Exercise 1

The grass **is** _____.

Porcupines **are** _____.

The doughnut **was** _____.

Exercise 2

The tractors were dusty.

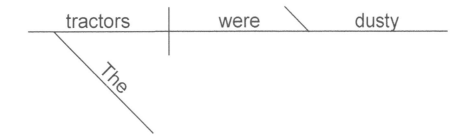

Exercise 3

1.   Tall gates are heavy.

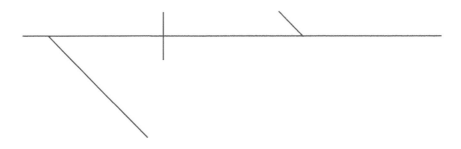

(Exercise 3 continues on the next page.)

Exercise 3 (continued)

2. Ten pigs were lazy.

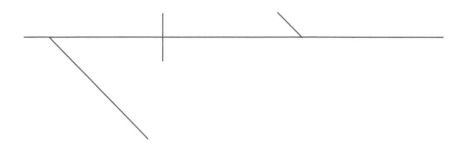

3. The Sahara Desert is dry.

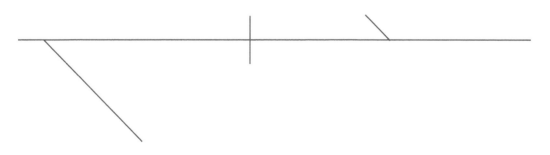

Exercise 4

I **am** Levi.

The queen **is** a ruler.

Pythons **are** snakes.

The man **was** a leader.

Exercise 5

Exercise 6

Pythons are snakes.

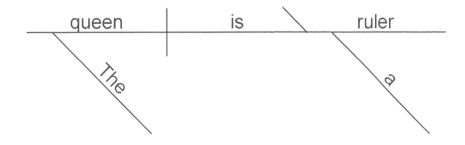

The queen is a ruler.

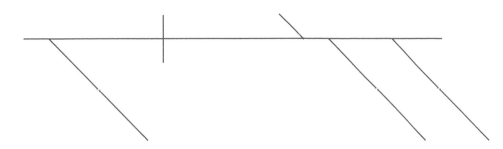

Exercise 7

1.   A platypus is an unusual mammal.

(Exercise 7 continues on the next page.)

2. Hermit crabs are amusing small pets.

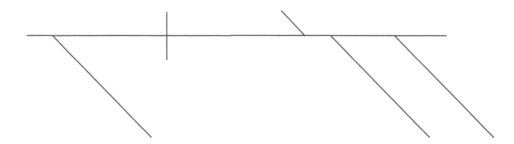

3. The Lincoln Memorial is a famous monument.

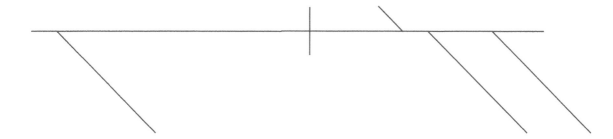

LESSON 39

Review: Common and Proper Nouns

Review: Forming Plurals

Exercise 1

Seasons
spring
summer
fall
winter

Exercise 2

Months of the Year	Days of the Week
January	Monday
February	Tuesday
March	Wednesday
April	Thursday
May	Friday
June	Saturday
July	Sunday
August	
September	
October	
November	
December	

Exercise 3

Roger Bannister

Roger Bannister ran.

Roger Bannister	ran

Exercise 4

1. Mount Rushmore is spectacular.

2. Saint Peter's Basilica is gigantic.

Exercise 5

●

desk

_____

kiss

_____

wish

_____

peach

_____

fox

_____

●

buzz

_____

sky

_____

holiday

_____

●

Exercise 6

Singular Noun	Plural Noun
child	children
foot	feet
tooth	teeth
man	men
woman	women
mouse	mice
goose	geese
deer	deer
fish	fish

Optional Follow-Up

Singular Noun	Plural Noun
child	
foot	
tooth	
man	
woman	
mouse	
goose	
deer	
fish	

LESSON 40

Exercise 1

Statements

I am a person.

You are my friend.

I like to run.

Trucks make noise.

Exercise 2

Commands

Stand up.

Stretch your hands into the air.

Make a silly face!

Hop up and down on one foot!

Exercise 3

Questions

Are we there yet?

How far do we have to go?

When do we eat?

May we turn up the radio?

Exercise 4

Exclamations

Our new puppy has stolen my shoe!

He is chewing it up!

That puppy is too sneaky!

I will definitely not leave my shoes out anymore!

Exercise 5

S = Statement   C = Command   Q = Question   E = Exclamation

1. Water covers almost three-quarters of the earth's surface. ____

2. Find the five oceans on your map. ____

3. What are the names of these oceans? ____

4. You are right! ____

5. The names of the oceans are the Pacific, Atlantic, Indian, Southern, and Arctic. ____

6. Water expands as it freezes. ____

7. Don't put a full bottle of water in the freezer. ____

8. Why not? ____

9. It might break the bottle! ____

10. The word "hippopotamus" means "river horse." ____

11. Picture that large animal in your mind. ____

12. Do you think the hippopotamus a kind of horse? ____

13. It is actually a type of pig! ____

14. Listen to this fact. ____

15. How much does an ostrich egg weigh? ____

16. It weighs three pounds. ____

17. That is a really heavy egg! ____

Optional Dictation Exercise

Optional Follow-Up

Hop on one foot.

Bark like a dog!

Walk backward.

Turn around three times.

Clap your hands behind your back.

Take three giant steps.

Sing a silly song!

Pretend you are a kangaroo.

134

LESSON 41

Exercise 1

Hannah runs.

Kernels pop.

Exercise 2

Run.

(you)	Run

Exercise 3

Look!

Walk quickly!

Exercise 4

Look!

Exercise 5

Walk quickly!

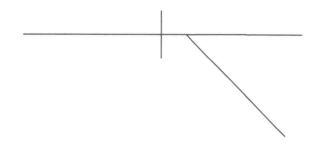

Dictation Exercise

_____ is the subject.

_____ is the subject.

_____ is the subject.

Optional Follow-Up

Sit down.

Stand up.

Walk across the room.

Pick up a book.

Tiptoe around the room.

Cluck like a chicken.

Clap your hands behind your back.

Hop on one foot.

Wiggle only two fingers.

LESSON 42

Exercise 1

John jumped.

John	jumped

Exercise 2

Jump.

(you)	Jump

Exercise 3

Study ancient history.

Wash the dishes!

138

Exercise 4

1.   Fred walked briskly.

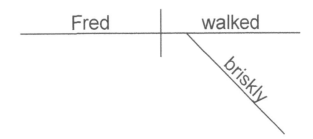

2.   Walk briskly.

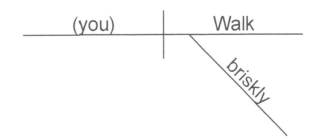

Exercise 5

Peg runs fast.

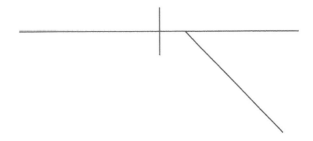

Run fast.

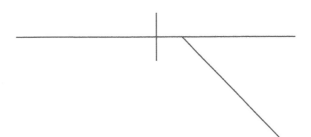

Exercise 6

Ray eats juicy pears.

Eat juicy pears.

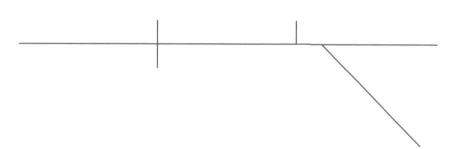

Exercise 7

Jane is polite.

Be polite.

Exercise 8

Brad breaks the ice.

Break the ice.

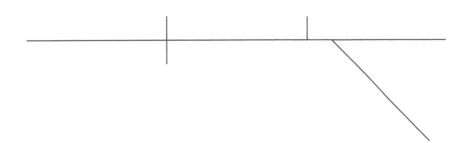

Optional Follow-Up

Giant plows pushed heavy snowdrifts aside.

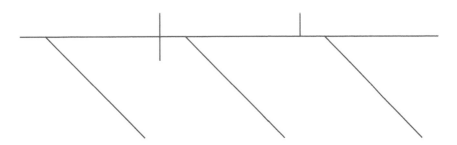

Little babies are often sleepy.

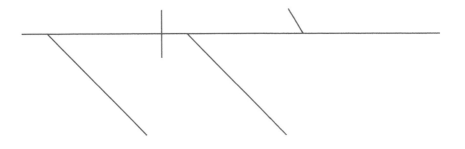

LESSON 43

I have recited the title, the author, and the poem.

☐ "The Land of Nod" by Robert Louis Stevenson

☐ "A Tragic Story" by William Makepeace Thackeray

☐ "I Wandered Lonely As a Cloud" by William Wordsworth

New: Questions (with Diagramming)

Exercise 1

Are they sitting?

Exercise 2

Are they sitting?

They are sitting.

Exercise 3

Can snakes swim?

Exercise 4

Can snakes swim?

Snakes can swim.

Exercise 5

1. Will Colin run?

2. May I play?

3. Could they clean?

4. Do whales sing?

5. Does ice float?

Exercise 6

1. Will Colin run? _____

   _____|_____

2. May I play? _____

   _____|_____

3. Could they clean? _____

   _____|_____

4. Do whales sing? _____

   _____|_____

5. Does ice float? _____

   _____|_____

LESSON 45

Exercise 1

I ate spinach earlier.

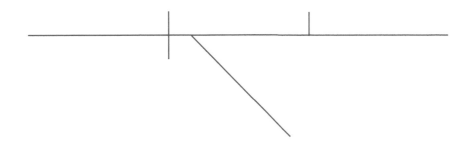

Exercise 2

Pass the cheese sauce.

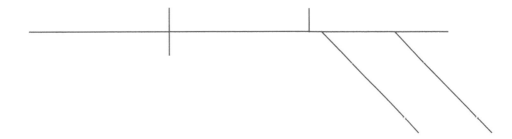

Exercise 3

Do you cook broccoli?

You do cook broccoli.

Exercise 4

Grandpa's chili is hot!

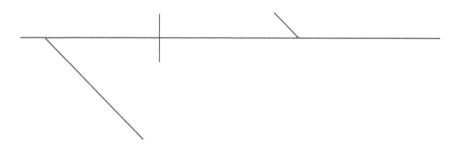

LESSON 46

A Time to Talk

by Robert Frost

When a friend calls to me from the road

And slows his horse to a meaning walk,

I don't stand still and look around

On all the hills I haven't hoed,

And shout from where I am, What is it?

No, not as there is a time to talk.

I thrust my hoe in the mellow ground,

Blade-end up and five feet tall,

And plod: I go up to the stone wall

For a friendly visit.

☐ **My instructor read the title, the author, and the poem to me. We talked about its meaning.**

Next we read the poem three times during the lesson.

☐ one

☐ two

☐ three

Later in the day we read the poem three times.

☐ one

☐ two

☐ three

And then we read the poem three more times.

☐ one

☐ two

☐ three

147

Dictation Exercise

LESSON 47

Review: Four Kinds of Verbs

Review: Direct Objects, Predicate Nominatives, and Predicate Adjectives

Exercise 1

Barb shook the blanket.

Cory forgave Greta.

Pedro licked a lollipop.

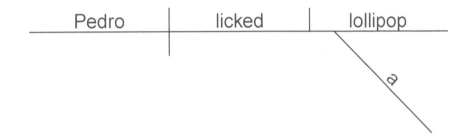

Exercise 2

Birds **will** chirp.

A flower **has** bloomed.

Bees **have** built a hive.

Exercise 3

I **am**.

He **was** here.

Our parents **were** in the kitchen, too.

Exercise 4

The verbs *am, is, are, was, were, be, being, been* can either

- help another verb
- show a state of being
- link two words together

Exercise 5

I am singing.

I am.

I am happy.

Exercise 6

Fleece **is** _____.

Gorillas **are** _____.

The macaroni **was** _____.

Exercise 7

Dancers are graceful.

Dancers | are \ graceful

Exercise 8

I am a boy.

I am a girl.

Exercise 9

Orlando is a city.

```
     Orlando    |    is    \    city
                 |          \
                            \
                             \ a
                              \
                               \
```

Dictation Exercise

_____

- -

_____

- -

_____

- -

_____

- -

_____

- -

_____

Optional Follow-Up

Spring is showery, flowery, bowery;

Summer is hoppy, croppy, poppy;

Autumn is wheezy, sneezy, freezy;

Winter is slippy, drippy, nippy.

LESSON 48

New: Prepositions

Exercise 1

Prepositions

Aboard, about, above, across.

After, against, along, among, around, at.

Before, behind, below, beneath.

Beside, between, beyond, by.

Down, during, except, for, from.

In, inside, into, like.

Near, of, off, on, over.

Past, since, through, throughout.

To, toward, under, underneath.

Until, up, upon.

With, within, without.

☐ **I have read the whole list of prepositions.**

☐ **I can say the first section from memory.**

Exercise 2

1. The captain aboard the ship whistles.

2. We read a story about bears.

3. The shelf above the desk holds books.

4. The house across the street is white.

Exercise 2 (continued)

5. The day after tomorrow is my birthday.

6. The rose against the fence is blooming.

7. The flowers along the road are yellow.

8. The clowns among the crowd made people laugh.

9. The store around the corner is huge.

10. The man at the door delivered a package.

Dictation Exercise

LESSON 49

Exercise 1

Prepositions

Aboard, about, above, across.

After, against, along, among, around, at.

Before, behind, below, beneath.

Beside, between, beyond, by.

Down, during, except, for, from.

In, inside, into, like.

Near, of, off, on, over.

Past, since, through, throughout.

To, toward, under, underneath.

Until, up, upon.

With, within, without.

☐ **I have read the whole list of prepositions.**

☐ **I can say the first section from memory.**

☐ **I can say the second section from memory.**

Exercise 2

1.   The presents <u>before her</u> were wrapped beautifully.

2.   The person <u>behind me</u> is last.

3.   The magma <u>below the surface</u> is boiling hot.

Exercise 2 (continued)

4. The fish <u>beneath the water</u> swim upstream.

5. I answered the phone beside the bed.

6. We hiked the mountain between the rivers.

7. The Pacific Ocean is the ocean beyond California.

8. Jacob will pick up those shoes by the door.

Dictation Exercise

LESSON 50

Exercise 1

Prepositions

Aboard, about, above, across.

After, against, along, among, around, at.

Before, behind, below, beneath.

Beside, between, beyond, by.

Down, during, except, for, from.

In, inside, into, like.

Near, of, off, on, over.

Past, since, through, throughout.

To, toward, under, underneath.

Until, up, upon.

With, within, without.

☐ **I have read the whole list of prepositions.**

☐ **I can say the first section from memory.**

☐ **I can say the second section from memory.**

☐ **I can say the third section from memory.**

Exercise 2

1. The cabin down the stream had no heat.

2. The blackout during the storm lasted three hours.

3. The whole family except the baby rode the rollercoaster.

4. My gift for you is a surprise.

5. The man from Idaho sells potatoes.

6. The woman in the black dress sang a solo.

7. The dishes inside the cabinet are fragile.

8. The path into the woods was shady.

9. A subject like arithmetic takes practice.

Dictation Exercise

New: Object of the Preposition

Exercise 1

Prepositions

Aboard, about, above, across.

After, against, along, among, around, at.

Before, behind, below, beneath.

Beside, between, beyond, by.

Down, during, except, for, from.

In, inside, into, like.

Near, of, off, on, over.

Past, since, through, throughout.

To, toward, under, underneath.

Until, up, upon.

With, within, without.

☐ **I have read the whole list of prepositions.**

☐ **I can say the first section from memory.**

☐ **I can say the second section from memory.**

☐ **I can say the third section from memory.**

☐ **I can say the fourth section from memory.**

Exercise 2

1. The lamp near the sofa is blue.

2. The capital of Virginia is Richmond.

3. The island off the coast is rocky.

4. The pancake on the griddle burned.

5. The black clouds over the city were frightening.

6. The town past Williamsburg is Yorktown.

7. The breeze through the window was cool.

8. The paintings throughout the museum were expensive.

Dictation Exercise

Review: Object of the Preposition

Exercise 1

Prepositions

Aboard, about, above, across.

After, against, along, among, around, at.

Before, behind, below, beneath.

Beside, between, beyond, by.

Down, during, except, for, from.

In, inside, into, like.

Near, of, off, on, over.

Past, since, through, throughout.

To, toward, under, underneath.

Until, up, upon.

With, within, without.

- ☐ **I have read the whole list of prepositions.**
- ☐ **I can say the first section from memory.**
- ☐ **I can say the second section from memory.**
- ☐ **I can say the third section from memory.**
- ☐ **I can say the fourth section from memory.**
- ☐ **I can say the fifth section from memory.**
- ☐ *CHALLENGE: I can say the whole list from memory while jumping on one foot.*

Exercise 2

1. He lost the key to his car.

2. His attitude toward his sister was helpful.

3. The kitten under the house was scared.

4. The suitcase underneath my bed is dusty.

5. The community pool up the street is open.

6. The frog upon the log croaked.

7. The lizard with the slender tail was green.

8. The hamster will nibble the food within the cage.

9. I would like ice cream without chocolate sauce.

Dictation Exercise

LESSON 53

Exercise 1

I drive the car with the dent.

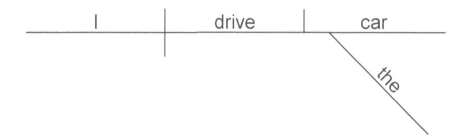

Exercise 2

1. We read a story about bears.

2. Shady paths in the woods are cool.

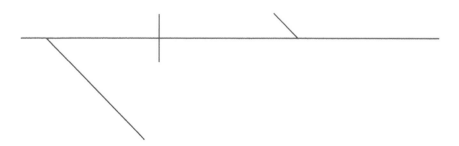

3.   The lamp near the sofa is blue.

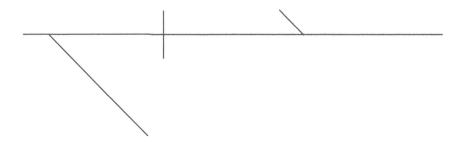

4.   Those pancakes on the griddle burned.

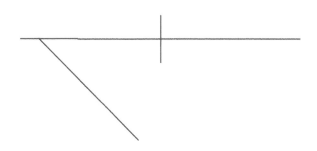

5.   He lost the key to his car.

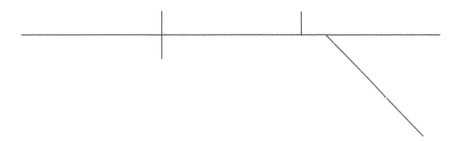

Exercise 3

In a treasure chest on the large, wooden ship across the harbor near the town, you will find a necklace with sparkling diamonds on it for the most beautiful queen in the whole world.

Isaac Newton's Laws of Gravity

One day, Isaac Newton was sitting beside a window, thinking and staring out into the family apple orchards, when he saw an apple fall to the ground. He thought, "Why does it always fall down? Why doesn't the apple ever fall sideways, or up? Some sort of force must be pulling on the apple to make it always fall in exactly the same way!"

Newton went on observing, doing experiments, and thinking until he was able to describe the force that pulls on the apple. He called it *gravity*, from the Latin word *grave*, which means "heavy." This "heavy" force means that large bodies, such as the earth, have a force that pulls objects toward them. Isaac Newton learned that he could predict, using mathematics, how strong the force would be, anywhere in the universe. The next time an apple fell, Newton could tell you exactly how fast it would fall and when it would hit the earth.

Newton's new rules, which we now call the laws of gravity, showed that every motion or action in the universe had a law that governed it. The universe wasn't a huge, mysterious, magical riddle. Instead, people could figure it out—and even predict ahead of time—what would happen.

LESSON 55

Exercise 1

green

sharp

spicy

enormous

sparkly

tasty

bumpy

ferocious

Exercise 2

this

that

these

those

first

third

next

final

Exercise 3

seventeen

four

fifty

most

several

another

all

Exercise 4

baby's

artist's

cat's

Dad's

Denise's

caterpillars'

pirates'

knights'

Exercise 5

Articles

Articles are little words,
You need know only three.
The articles that describe nouns
are **a**, **an**, **the**.

Exercise 6

An octopus propels through the water

An armadillo is a mammal.

The Egyptian pharaoh Hatshepsut was really a woman!

Exercise 7

Monkeys chatter.

The lively monkeys chatter.

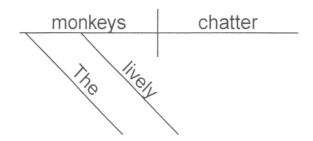

Exercise 8

1. Trees' last brown leaves drop.

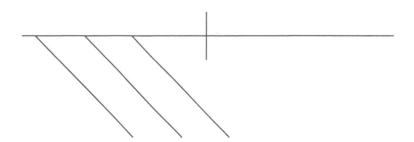

2. The third gigantic bubble burst.

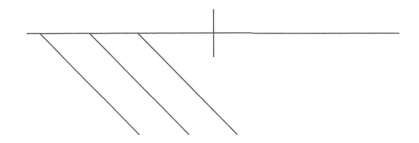

3. All soft, golden daffodils sway.

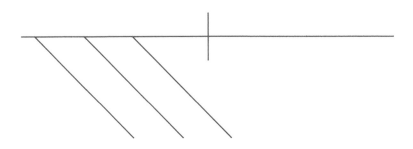

4. Harold's two rusty cars rattle.

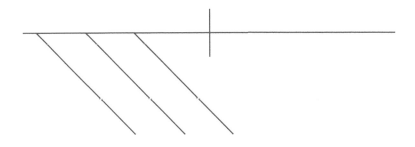

5. Students' heavy blue backpacks drooped.

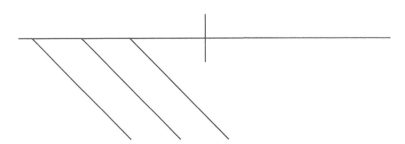

169

Optional Follow-Up

Flowers are red.

People were happy.

Two boys are being wild.

My cousins have been angry.

All the dogs should be hungry.

LESSON 56

Exercise 1

I sing **quietly**.

I sing **happily**.

I sing **beautifully**.

I sing **clearly**.

I sing **loudly**.

Exercise 2

quickly

quietly

slowly

loudly

I walk _____.

Exercise 3

I sing **today**.

I sing **tonight**.

I sing **late**.

I sing **early**.

I sing **now**.

Exercise 4

today

tonight

late

now

I sleep _____.

Exercise 5

I read **nearby**.

I read **outside**.

I read **upstairs**.

I read **here**.

I read **everywhere**.

Exercise 6

outdoors

nearby

here

I swim _____.

172

Exercise 7

I wash **daily**.

I wash **rarely**.

I wash **seldom**.

I wash **frequently**.

I wash **often**.

Exercise 8

yearly

frequently

rarely

I camp _____.

Exercise 9

1. Leopards creep gingerly.

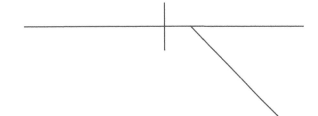

2. Dolphins swam alongside.

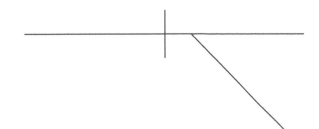

(Exercise 9 continues on the next page.)

3.   Foxes sneak slyly.

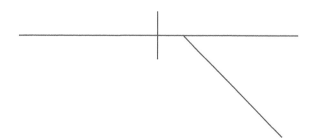

4.   Dad left early.

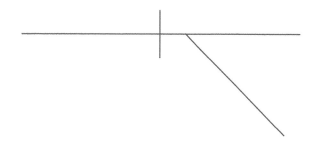

5.   Dragonflies can fly backward.

6.   Thomas Alva Edison napped frequently.

Promises for the Day

1. I will make my bed _____ .

    soon

    later

    tomorrow

2. I will walk across the room _____ .

    quickly

    gracefully

    sleepily

3. I will read a book _____ .

    inside

    nearby

    there

4. I will eat my snack _____ .

    slowly

    greedily

    later

5. I will hug someone _____ .

    now

    today

    tenderly

I hereby promise to do all the activities above, exactly as I have stated.

_____   _____
Student Signature   Signature of Witness (Instructor)

LESSON 57

Exercise 1

I will jump excitedly.

I will jump immediately.

I will jump outside.

I will jump daily.

Exercise 2

too

very

really

quite

slightly

Exercise 3

too gentle

very gentle

really gentle

quite gentle

slightly gentle

Exercise 4

Donkeys are too stubborn!

Donkeys | are \ stubborn
                          too

Exercise 5

1. Firemen are very courageous.

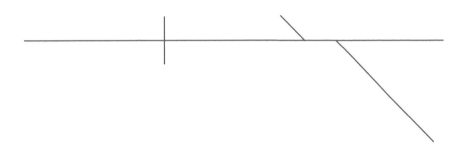

2. George was really curious.

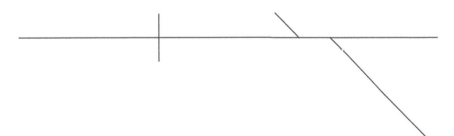

3. Insects are quite fascinating.

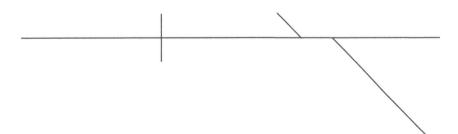

(Exercise 5 continues on the next page.)

Exercise 5 (continued)

4.   They were slightly nervous.

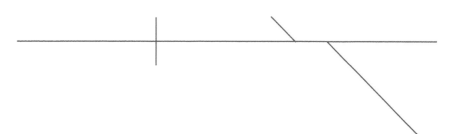

Exercise 6

too

very

really

quite

slightly

Exercise 7

too early

very early

really early

quite early

slightly early

Exercise 8

Rain came very suddenly.

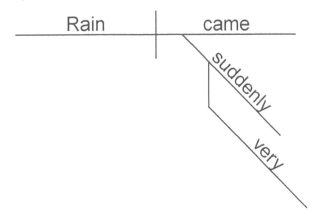

Exercise 9

1. Arnold slept slightly late.

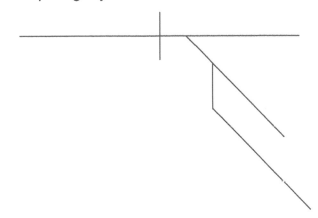

2. Kris skated too fast.

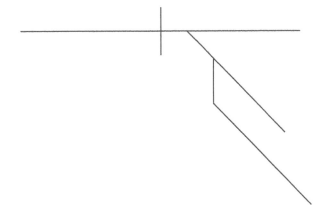

(Exercise 9 continues on the next page.)

3.   Garcia stopped really quickly.

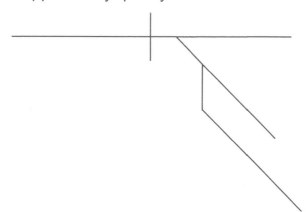

4.   Ravens caw quite loudly.

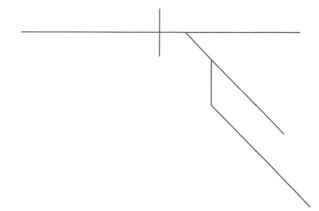

Optional Follow-Up

● too

very

really

quite

slightly

1. The clown was _____ **silly**.

2. The hamburger was _____ **big**!

3. The baby is _____ **ticklish**.

4. I arrived _____ **late**.

5. I ate my ice cream _____ **quickly**.

● 6. The puppy was _____ **friendly**.

●

The Bells
by Edgar Allan Poe

Hear the sledges with the bells—

Silver bells!

What a world of merriment their melody foretells!

How they tinkle, tinkle, tinkle,

In the icy air of night!

While the stars that oversprinkle

All the heavens, seem to twinkle

With a crystalline delight;

Keeping time, time, time,

In a sort of Runic rhyme,

To the tintinnabulation, that so musically wells

From the bells, bells, bells, bells,

Bells, bells, bells—

From the jingling and the tingling of the bells.

☐ My instructor read the title, the author, and the poem to me. We talked about its meaning.

Next we read the poem three times during the lesson.

☐ one

☐ two

☐ three

Later in the day we read the poem three times.

☐ one

☐ two

☐ three

And then we read the poem three more times.

☐ one

☐ two

☐ three

Dictation Exercise

LESSON 59

Exercise 1

Max opened the door.

The waiter serves dinner.

Charles found Dave.

Charles	found	Dave

Exercise 2

Carmen **shall** sleep.

The frogs **are** hiding.

We **have been** playing.

Exercise 3

We **are** in the room.

Anton has **been** to the city.

The actors will **be** on stage.

Exercise 4

The verbs *am, is, are, was, were, be, being, been* can either

- help another verb
- show a state of being
- link two words together

184

Exercise 5

He was climbing.

He was on a mountain.

He was patient.

Exercise 6

Popcorn **is** _____.

Marbles **are** _____.

The clay **was** _____.

Exercise 7

The costumes were fancy.

Exercise 8

I will **be** a veterinarian.

I will **be** an astronaut.

I will **be** a builder.

Exercise 9

Teri is a nurse.

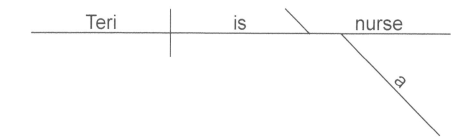

Dictation Exercise

Optional Follow-Up

Subject	Verb	Predicate Adjective
Spring	will be	warm
Summer	should be	snowy
Autumn	can be	busy
Winter	was	fun
		rainy
		freezing
		sunny
		breezy

LESSON 60

Review: Simple and Complete Subjects and Predicates

Exercise 1

Hardworking Marie plants many flowers outside.

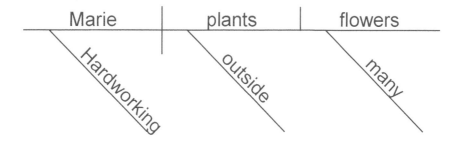

Exercise 2

Two sheepdogs herd wandering sheep efficiently.

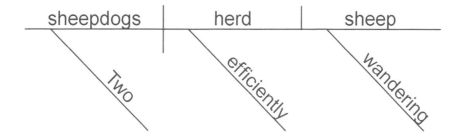

Exercise 3

Hardworking Marie plants many flowers outside.

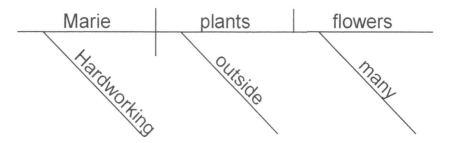

188

Exercise 4

Astronauts fly spacecrafts.

Brave astronauts fly spacecrafts.

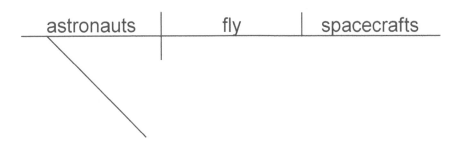

Brave astronauts fly sleek spacecrafts.

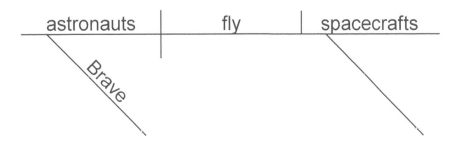

Brave astronauts fly sleek spacecrafts yearly.

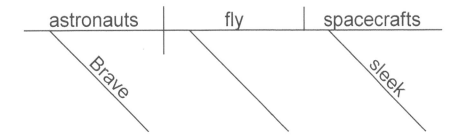

Exercise 5

Astronomers watch clouds.

Observant astronomers watch clouds.

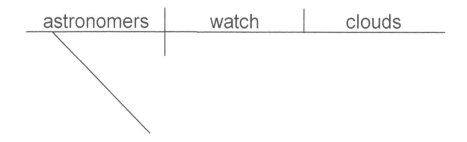

Observant astronomers watch Martian clouds.

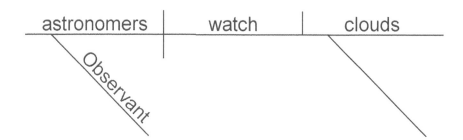

Observant astronomers watch Martian clouds closely.

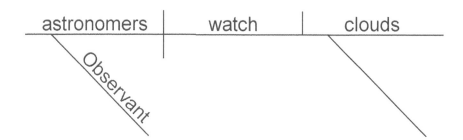

Exercise 6

Flares blast energy.

Solar flares blast energy.

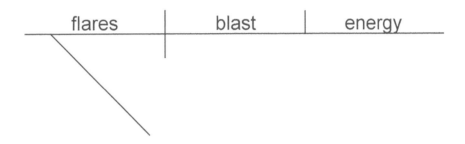

Solar flares blast magnetic energy.

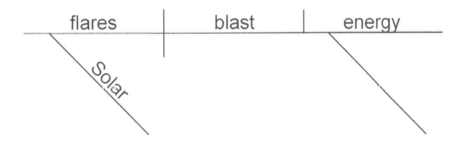

Solar flares blast magnetic energy suddenly.

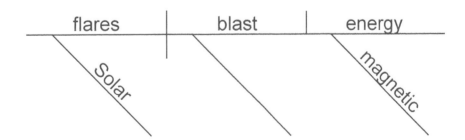

Group 1

Currents carved canyons.

Undersea currents carved canyons.

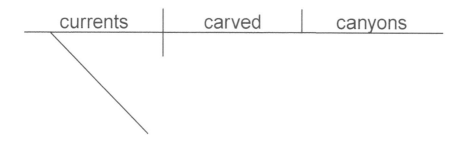

Undersea currents carved submarine canyons.

currents | carved | canyons
Undersea

Undersea currents carved submarine canyons gradually.

currents | carved | canyons
Undersea *submarine*

Group 2

Volcanoes ooze lava.

Submarine volcanoes ooze lava.

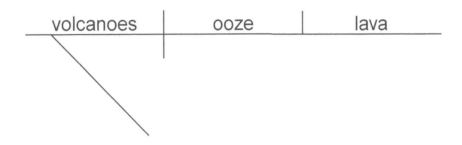

Submarine volcanoes ooze hot lava.

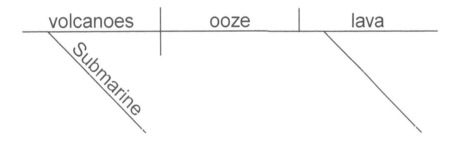

Submarine volcanoes ooze hot lava underwater.

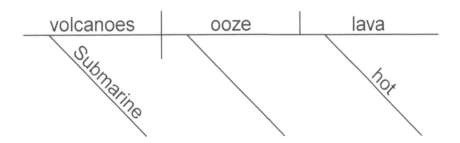

LESSON 61

New: Initials and Abbreviations for Titles of Respect

New: Abbreviations for Months and Days of the Week

Exercise 1

1. _____

2. _____

3. _____

4. _____

5. _____

6. _____

7. _____

8. _____

Exercise 2

Title of Respect	Abbreviation	Used For
Mister	Mr.	a man
Mistress	Mrs.	a married woman
Doctor	Dr.	a physician
Miss	—	an unmarried girl or woman
Mistress or Miss	Ms.	You should use Ms. when you do not know whether a woman would prefer to be called Mrs. or Miss.

Exercise 3

Exercise 4

Monday	Mon.	
Tuesday	Tue.	
Wednesday	Wed.	
Thursday	Thu.	
Friday	Fri.	
Saturday	Sat.	
Sunday	Sun.	

Exercise 5

Monday	
Tuesday	
Wednesday	
Thursday	
Friday	
Saturday	
Sunday	

Exercise 6

January	Jan.	
February	Feb.	
March	Mar.	
April	Apr.	
May	—	
June	—	
July	—	
August	Aug.	
September	Sept.	
October	Oct.	
November	Nov.	
December	Dec.	

Exercise 7

January	
February	
March	
April	
May	
June	
July	
August	
September	
October	
November	
December	

LESSON 62

Exercise 1

and

but

or

Exercise 2

Rabbits **and** hamsters eat lettuce.

Fish **and** tadpoles swim.

I can run **and** jump.

Dogs can bark **and** bite.

Exercise 3

You may play **or** read.

You may eat eggs **or** cheese.

Jim **or** Leslie should stay.

Cyclists **or** joggers may use this lane.

Exercise 4

I am <u>tired</u> **but** <u>happy</u>.

<u>I want to go outside</u>, **but** <u>I cannot find my coat</u>.

<u>I would eat my spinach</u>, **but** <u>I am not hungry</u>.

Exercise 5

My dog and cat are friends.

The children will work or play.

Exercise 6

Jan runs.

Mel skips.

Jan runs, but Mel skips.

Exercise 7

1. I will give you the cookie and the milk.

2. I will give you the cookie and the milk and the apple and the napkin.

3. I will give you the cookie, the milk, the apple, and the napkin.

Exercise 8

1. I am going to play baseball. I need a ball, a bat, a glove, and a helmet.

2. I am making cookies. I mix flour, sugar, butter, vanilla, and eggs.

3. I went to the zoo. I saw tigers, elephants, lions, monkeys, and snakes.

Exercise 9

1. Plants need water, sunshine, and fertilizer.

2. People need food, water, and sleep.

3. You can see the moon, stars, planets, and comets in the night sky.

Exercise 10

I mix flour and sugar.

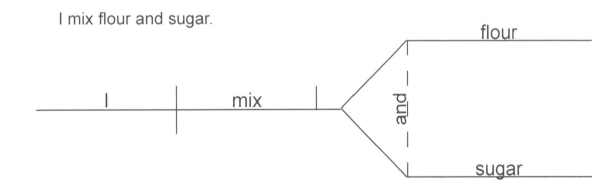

1.　I mix flour, sugar, butter, vanilla, and eggs.

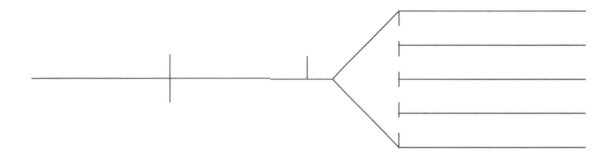

2.　He invited Burt, Max, Bob, Tom, and Jed.

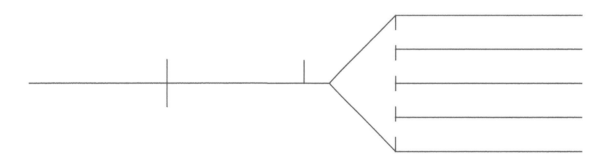

3.　She owns cats, dogs, fish, birds, lizards, and frogs.

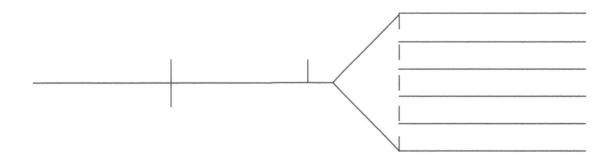

LESSON 63

Exercise 1

1. I will give my brother a book and a stuffed animal and a toy car and Legos.

2. I will give my brother a book, a stuffed animal, a toy car, and Legos.

Exercise 2

1. Alan, Carrie, Lucy, and I are playing together this afternoon.

2. Mother will make snacks for Alan, Carrie, Lucy, and me.

3. Jimmy, Joseph, and he went to the game with me.

(Exercise 2 continues on the next page.)

203

Exercise 2 (continued)

4.   I went to the game with Jimmy, Joseph, and him.

Exercise 3

Kathy, please get me a dishcloth.

Hazel, are you ready to start to work?

New: Contractions

Exercise 1

AM

I am	→	I am	→	I'm

IS

he is	→	he is	→	he's
she is	→	she is	→	she's
it is	→	it is	→	it's

ARE

we are	→	we are	→	we're
you are	→	you are	→	you're
they are	→	they are	→	they're

HAVE

I have	→	I have	→	I've
you have	→	you have	→	you've
we have	→	we have	→	we've
they have	→	they have	→	they've

HAS

he has	→	he has	→	he's
she has	→	she has	→	she's
it has	→	it has	→	it's

HAD

I had	→	I had	→	I'd
you had	→	you had	→	you'd
he had	→	he had	→	he'd
she had	→	she had	→	she'd
it had	→	it had	→	it'd
we had	→	we had	→	we'd
they had	→	they had	→	they'd

(Exercise 1 continues on the next page.)

WILL

I will	→	I will	→	I'll
you will	→	you will	→	you'll
he will	→	he will	→	he'll
she will	→	she will	→	she'll
it will	→	it will	→	it'll
we will	→	we will	→	we'll
they will	→	they will	→	they'll

WOULD

I would	→	I would	→	I'd
you would	→	you would	→	you'd
he would	→	he would	→	he'd
she would	→	she would	→	she'd
it would	→	it would	→	it'd
we would	→	we would	→	we'd
they would	→	they would	→	they'd

LET

let us	→	let us	→	let's

NEGATIVE CONTRACTIONS

_____ NOT

is not	→	is not	→	isn't
are not	→	are not	→	aren't
was not	→	was not	→	wasn't
were not	→	were not	→	weren't
have not	→	have not	→	haven't
has not	→	has not	→	hasn't
had not	→	had not	→	hadn't
do not	→	do not	→	don't
does not	→	does not	→	doesn't
did not	→	did not	→	didn't
should not	→	should not	→	shouldn't
would not	→	would not	→	wouldn't
can not	→	can not	→	can't
could not	→	could not	→	couldn't
will not	→	will not	→	won't

Exercise 2

1. **We will** eat lunch soon.

2. **It is** almost noon.

3. **You are** eating with us.

4. Antonia **could not** come.

5. She **will not** be in town.

LESSON 65

I have recited the title, the author, and the poem.

☐ "The Land of Nod" by Robert Louis Stevenson

☐ "A Tragic Story" by William Makepeace Thackeray

☐ "I Wandered Lonely As a Cloud" by William Wordsworth

☐ "A Time to Talk" by Robert Frost

☐ "The Bells" by Edgar Allan Poe

LESSON 66

Narration: "Spiders"

Spiders

Spiders are one of the marvels of the animal world and do not deserve the aversion and fear some persons feel for them. They are beneficial to mankind, for they destroy vast numbers of flies, mosquitoes, and other injurious insects; and since all but two harm neither human beings nor plants, they should not be killed.

Usually spiders have eight eyes on the front part of the head, although some species have one, two, or three pairs of eyes, and those living in caves are often entirely blind. The spider has a pair of jaws that are modified antennae; with these the prey is caught and poison is injected into the body, which is later mangled and the juices sucked out.

LESSON 67

Exercise 1

The truck could go nowhere.

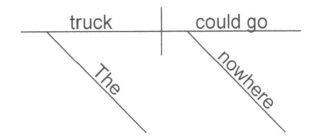

Exercise 2

Rita never fears the dark.

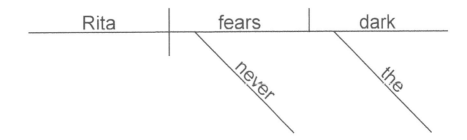

Exercise 3

You should not feed the animals.

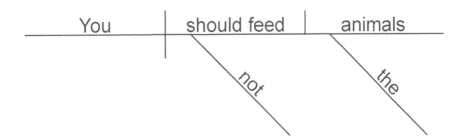

Exercise 4

You shouldn't feed the animals.

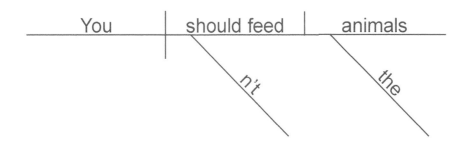

Exercise 5

1. Jeremy hasn't jumped.

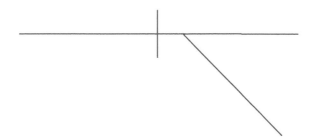

2. I don't swim.

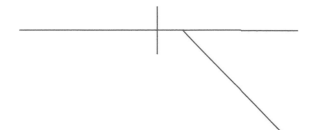

Exercise 6

1. I **will not** tease.

   -

2. Babies **can not** walk.

   -

3. **It is** cold today.

   -

4. **We would** like to have dinner.

   -

5. **You have** finished the book.

   -

Exercise 7

1. **She will** come with us.

   _____

2. **I am** happy.

   _____

3. **They are** my friends.

   _____

(Exercise 7 continues on the next page.)

Exercise 7 (continued)

4. **Was not** she here earlier?

    _____

5. **Do not** feed the animals.

    _____

Optional Follow-Up

1. Penguins can't fly.

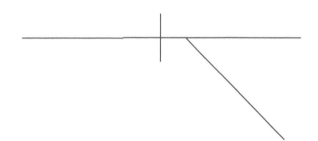

2. Corey doesn't type.

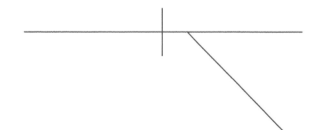

LESSON 68

Exercise 1

1. Tuesday is a day of the week.   Statement

2. Pick up all of your toys.   Command

3. Will I need my snow boots?   Question

4. This box is too heavy!   Exclamation

Exercise 2

S = Statement   C = Command   Q = Question   E = Exclamation

1. Put away your toy trucks. ____

2. I need help right away! ____

3. Is my blue coat in the closet? ____

4. I have one birthday each year. ____

5. Put the lid on the jar. ____

6. Whew, I am glad that is over! ____

7. February is the second month of the year. ____

8. Is our picnic lunch packed in the car? ____

Exercise 3

Mother asked, **"Did you wash your hands?"**

The children chanted together, **"We did."**

Dad said, **"Sit down."**

Carmen exclaimed, **"I am so hungry!"**

Exercise 4

1. Mother asked**,** **"**Did you wash your hands**?"**

2. The children chanted together**,** **"**We did**."**

3. Dad said**,** **"**Sit down**."**

4. Carmen exclaimed**,** **"**I am so hungry**!"**

Exercise 5

1. Mother asked, "Did you wash your hands?"

2. The children chanted together, "We did."

3. Dad said, "Sit down."

4. Carmen exclaimed, "I am so hungry!"

Exercise 6

1. Mohandas Gandhi said, "Where there is love, there is life."

----

2. Patrick Henry cried, "Give me liberty or give me death!"

----

3. Saint Paul asked, "If God is for us, who can be against us?"

Optional Follow-Up

Jody said I ate all of the cake.

Jody said, "I ate all of the cake."

The children cried today.

The children cried, "Today!"

The duke declared I am now the king!

The duke declared, "I am now the king!"

LESSON 69

Exercise 1

I play soccer weekly.

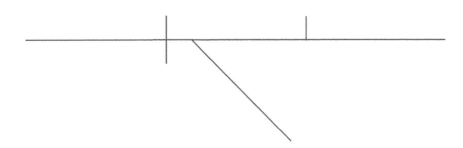

Exercise 2

Kick the soccer ball.

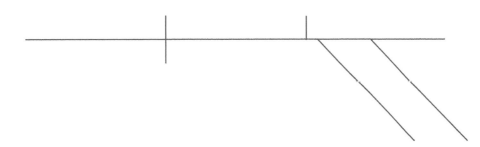

Exercise 3

Do you play soccer?

You do play soccer.

Exercise 4

Brent's kicks were hard!

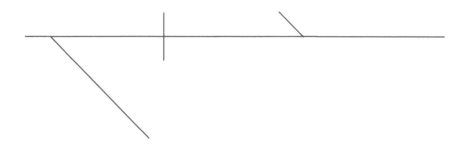

Exercise 5

"**Did you wash your hands?**" Mother asked.

"**We did,**" the children chanted together.

"**Sit down,**" Dad said.

"**I am so hungry!**" Carmen exclaimed.

Exercise 6

1.   "Did you wash your hands?" Mother asked.

_____

2.   "We did," the children chanted together.

_____

3.   "Sit down," Dad said.

_____

4.   "I am so hungry!" Carmen exclaimed.

_____

Exercise 7

1.   "Did you wash your hands?" Mother asked.

2.   "We did," the children chanted together.

3.   "Sit down," Dad said.

4.   "I am so hungry!" Carmen exclaimed.

Exercise 8

1. "No great thing is created suddenly," said Epictetus.

_____

_____

_____

_____

2. "Sing a song of seasons!" wrote Robert Louis Stevenson.

_____

_____

_____

_____

3. "Can two walk together, except they be agreed?" God asked Amos.

_____

_____

_____

_____

Optional Follow-Up

The king/queen ordered, "No, you may not!"

"Yes, you have my permission," granted the king/queen.

The king/queen asked, "Why should I allow you to do that?"

LESSON 70

Exercise 1

Betty asked, **"May we make cookies?"**

Mother said, **"Get out the ingredients."**

Ralph stated, **"We will use butter, flour, and sugar."**

Betty exclaimed, **"Sugar cookies are my favorite!"**

Exercise 2

1. Betty asked, "May we make cookies?"

   _____

   _____

   _____

2. Mother said, "Get out the ingredients."

   _____

   _____

   _____

3. Ralph stated, "We will use butter, flour, and sugar."

   _____

   _____

   _____

4. Betty exclaimed, "Sugar cookies are my favorite!"

   _____

   _____

   _____

Exercise 3

"**May we make cookies?**" Betty asked.

"**Get out the ingredients,**" Mother said.

"**We will use butter, flour, and sugar,**" Ralph stated.

"**Sugar cookies are my favorite!**" Betty exclaimed.

Exercise 4

1. "May we make cookies?" Betty asked.

---

2. "Get out the ingredients," Mother said.

---

3. "We will use butter, flour, and sugar," Ralph stated.

---

4. "Sugar cookies are my favorite!" Betty exclaimed.

Exercise 5

1. "May we make cookies?" Betty asked.

   Betty asked if Mother would let her and Ralph make cookies.

2. Mother said, "Get out the ingredients."

   Mother told Betty to get out the ingredients.

3. "We will use butter, flour, and sugar," Ralph stated.

   Ralph said that they would use butter, flour, and sugar to make
   the cookies.

4. Betty exclaimed, "Sugar cookies are my favorite!"

   Betty exclaimed that sugar cookies were her favorite.

Optional Follow-Up

1. "The only thing we have to fear is fear itself," asserted Franklin
   Roosevelt.

2. Christina Rossetti stated, "There is no friend like a sister."

3. Socrates exclaimed, "How many things I can do without!"

4. "The supreme happiness in life is the conviction that we are loved,"
   said Victor Hugo.

5. Henry David Thoreau once said, "Our life is frittered away by
   detail … Simplify, simplify."

LESSON 71

A Slash of Blue
by Emily Dickinson

A slash of Blue —

A sweep of Gray —

Some scarlet patches on the way,

Compose an Evening Sky —

A little purple — slipped between —

Some Ruby Trousers hurried on —

A Wave of Gold —

A Bank of Day —

This just makes out the Morning Sky.

☐ **My instructor read the title, the author, and the poem to me. We talked about its meaning.**

Next we read the poem three times during the lesson.

☐ one

☐ two

☐ three

Later in the day we read the poem three times.

☐ one

☐ two

☐ three

And then we read the poem three more times.

☐ one

☐ two

☐ three

226

LESSON 72

Review: Commas in a Series and in Direct Address

Review: Contractions

Exercise 1

1.   I will lend you a baseball **and** a mitt.

2.   I will lend you a baseball **and** a mitt **and** a helmet **and** a bat.

3.   I will lend you a baseball, a mitt, a helmet, and a bat.

Exercise 2

1.   I am going shopping. I will buy bananas, milk, eggs, and bread.

2.   I set up a terrarium today. I collected beetles, ants, moths, crickets,

     and butterflies.

3.   I went to the park. It has a pond, a soccer field, swings, bike paths,

     and picnic tables.

Exercise 3

1. Dolphins, whales, and manatees are mammals that live in the ocean.

2. Glue can be made from animal bones, fish, milk, or vegetables.

3. We grow tomatoes, peppers, and herbs in our garden.

Exercise 4

Katie, please set the table.

Margaret, did you wash your hands?

Exercise 5

1. I am _____

2. it is _____

3. she would _____

4. you are _____

5. he will _____

6. they have _____

7. I will _____

8. it has _____

9. does not _____

10. will not _____

Exercise 6

1. **We have** eaten already.

2. **It has** been a pleasant day.

3. **Let us** leave for our camping trip now.

4. He **is not** late.

5. I **should not** bother a wasp nest.

Review: Prepositions

Review: Conjunctions

Exercise 1

Prepositions

Aboard, about, above, across.

After, against, along, among, around, at.

Before, behind, below, beneath.

Beside, between, beyond, by.

Down, during, except, for, from.

In, inside, into, like.

Near, of, off, on, over.

Past, since, through, throughout.

To, toward, under, underneath.

Until, up, upon.

With, within, without.

☐ **I have read the whole list of prepositions.**
☐ **I can say the first section from memory.**
☐ **I can say the second section from memory.**
☐ **I can say the third section from memory.**
☐ **I can say the fourth section from memory.**
☐ **I can say the fifth section from memory.**
☐ ***CHALLENGE: I can say the whole list from memory while spinning around and NOT falling down.***

Exercise 2

and

but

or

Exercise 3

<u>Pencils</u> **and** <u>crayons</u> can be sharpened.

<u>Multiplication</u> **and** <u>division</u> take practice.

I study <u>Latin</u> **and** <u>Spanish</u>.

I can <u>write</u> **and** <u>spell</u>.

Exercise 4

<u>Sherry</u> **or** <u>Jackie</u> will go with us.

<u>Skip</u> **or** <u>walk</u> around the park.

You may wear a <u>sweater</u> **or** <u>jacket</u>.

We will collect <u>shells</u> **or** <u>rocks</u>.

Exercise 5

The steak was <u>large</u> **but** <u>tender</u>.

The trip was <u>long</u> **but** <u>fun</u>.

<u>I will play the guitar</u>, **but** <u>I will take my violin with me</u>.

<u>Our house is small</u>, **but** <u>it is comfortable</u>.

Exercise 6

1. My sister and brother are twins.

2. The lady hums or sings.

Exercise 7

Jo hides.

Keith seeks.

Jo hides, but Keith seeks.

Dictation Exercise

LESSON 74

Exercise 1

Emily sings.

Emily and Ella sing.

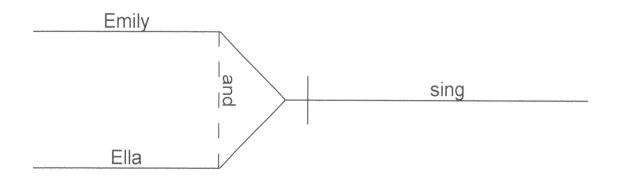

Exercise 2

1.   Fish and tadpoles swim.

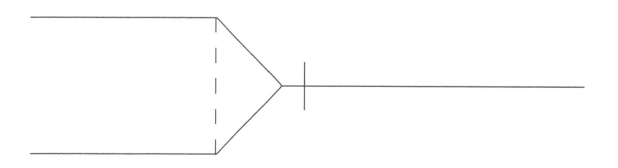

2. Birds and bees fly.

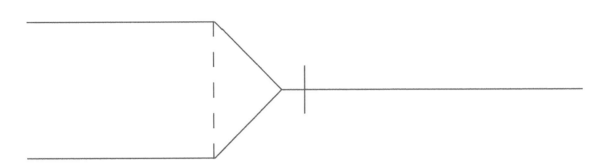

3. Ted and Mark jog.

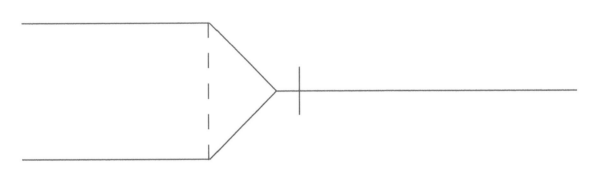

4. Balls and marbles roll.

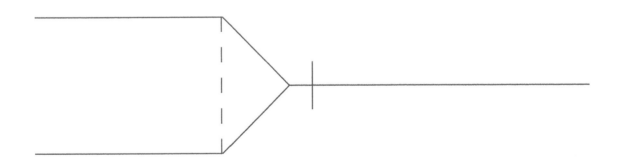

Optional Dictation Exercise

LESSON 75

New: Compound Verbs (with Diagramming)

Review: Prepositional Phrases

Exercise 1

Emily sings.

Emily sings and plays.

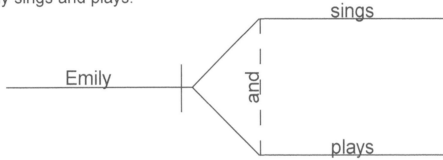

Exercise 2

1. Snakes hiss and slither.

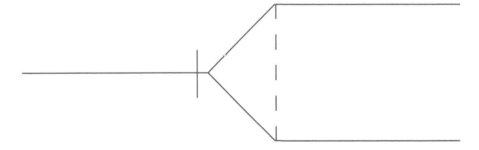

2. Wind whistles and whines.

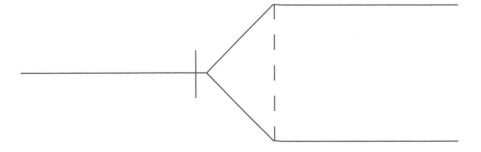

(Exercise 2 continues on the next page.)

3.   Brooks tumble and swirl.

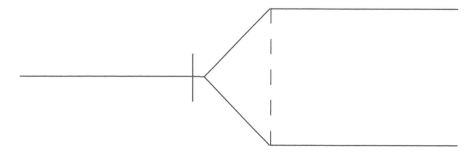

4.   Soup bubbles and boils.

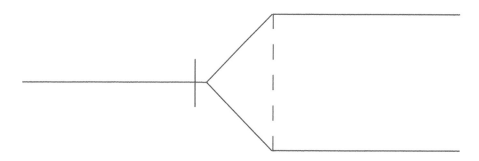

Exercise 3

Here are the keys to the car.

Exercise 4

1.   His kindness toward the baby was sweet.

2.   The closet under the stairs was tiny.

3.   There are many bugs underneath the rock.

4.   The kitten up the tree is scared.

Exercise 5

In the pasture on the old farm by the banks of the James River, a horse

nibbles grass near the edge of the rickety fence with chipped white paint on it.

LESSON 76

Exercise 1

Sausage and bacon sizzle.

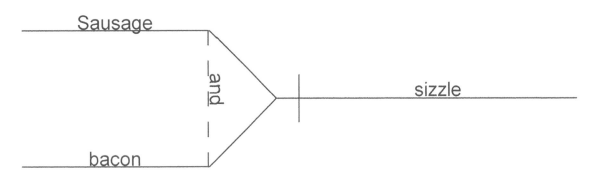

Exercise 2

Roads twist and turn.

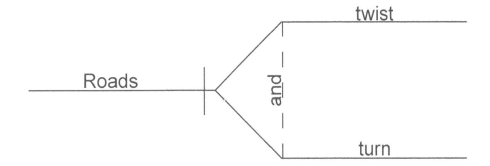

Exercise 3

Tulips and daffodils flutter and dance.

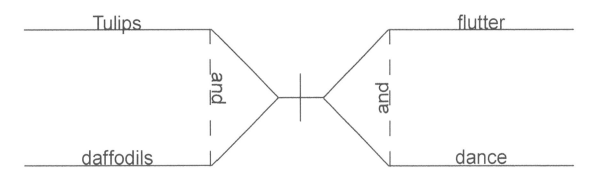

Exercise 4

1. Swallows and martins dart and swoop.

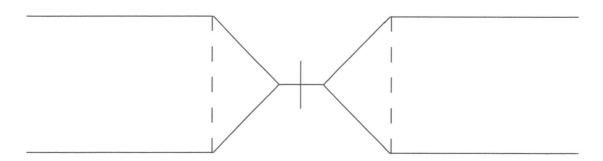

2. Walter and Brenda read and write.

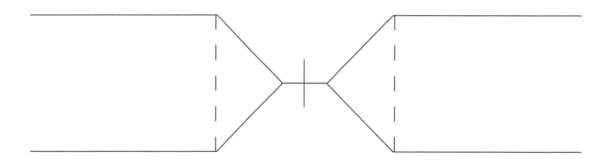

3. Bees and wasps fly and sting.

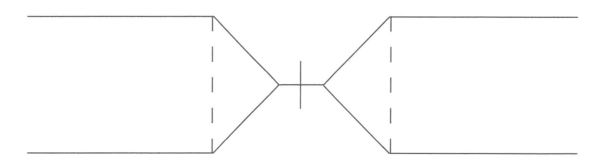

Bull-Jumpers in Early Crete

If you were a boy or girl in ancient Crete, you might find yourself part of a bull-jumping team! The Minoans, who lived on the island of Crete, trained athletic children to become bull-jumpers. The children learned the kind of gymnastics that children still learn today—somersaulting, balance exercises, tumbling, and vaulting. But instead of doing their vaulting over a piece of equipment, the students learned how to vault over the backs of small animals such as goats—and then finally were taught how to leap over the backs of bulls.

During bull-jumping festivals, people came from all over Crete to cheer for the bull-jumpers. Bull-jumpers were treated like royalty. They were given the best food and the nicest places to live. They were showered with presents of gold, jewelry, and beautiful clothes. But bull-jumping was a dangerous sport, because bull-jumpers were often killed by the bulls they were supposed to leap over. Few bull-jumpers lived past the age of twenty.

LESSON 78

Exercise 1

1. Beowulf battled monsters.

2. The monster destroys the door.

3. A dragon bites Beowulf.

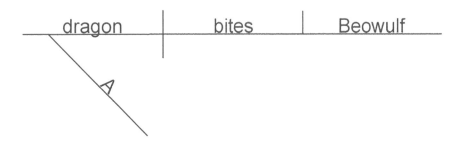

Exercise 2

1. The violins **should** tune.

2. The horns **will be** sounding.

3. The drums **did** beat.

243

Exercise 3

1. The violins **are** in the front.

2. The horn players **were** backstage.

3. The conductor **is** on the podium.

Exercise 4

The verbs *am, is, are, was, were, be, being, been* can either

- help another verb
- show a state of being
- link two words together

Exercise 5

1. Daniel is practicing.

2. Daniel is in the orchestra.

3. Daniel is a boy.

4. Daniel is talented.

Exercise 6

Pretzels **are** _____.

The kaleidoscope **was** _____.

The hamster **is** _____.

Exercise 7

1. The weather is gloomy.

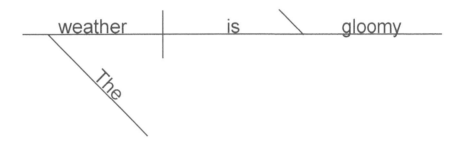

2. Simon was the winner.

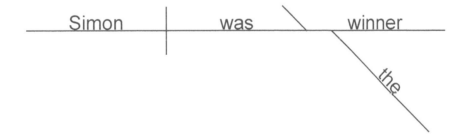

1.   Monsters destroyed the door.

2.   A dragon will bite Beowulf.

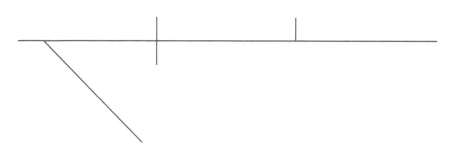

3.   I am.

4.   Salty pretzels are yummy.

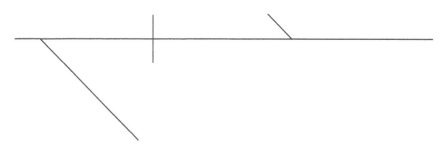

5.   Mother is a teacher.

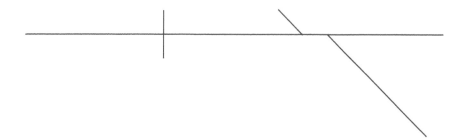

LESSON 79

Exercise 1

gentle

sugary

silly

dangerous

Exercise 2

this

those

second

last

Exercise 3

ten

many

several

all

Exercise 4

baby's

teacher's

Dad's

librarians'

Exercise 5

Articles

Articles are little words,

You need know only three.

The articles that describe nouns

are **a**, **an**, **the**.

Exercise 6

An eagle steals a fish from another bird.

The oil in a shark's liver helps it to float.

The actress Theodora became an empress.

Exercise 7

young seal

younger seal

youngest seal

Exercise 8

There are three beds in my house.

Papa Bear's bed is **soft**.

Mama Bear's bed is **softer**.

Baby Bear's bed is the **softest**.

Pythons vary in size.

A **large** python can swallow a monkey.

A **larger** python can swallow a deer.

The **largest** python could swallow a person!

The crane fly is **small**.

The robber fly is **smaller**.

Midges are the **smallest** fly of the three.

The Arctic Ocean is **wide**.

The Atlantic Ocean is **wider**.

The Pacific Ocean is the **widest** ocean of all.

Exercise 9

1. This gecko is green.

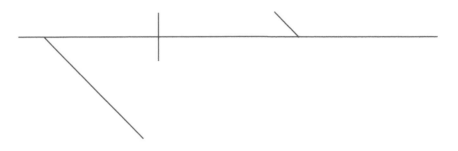

2. A greener gecko scurries.

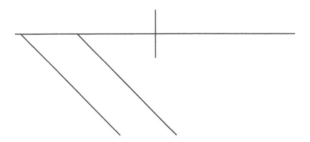

3. The greenest gecko hides.

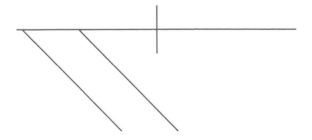

Dictation Exercise

Optional Follow-Up

big

bigger

biggest

long

longer

longest

new

newer

newest

250

Review: Adverbs

Exercise 1

I draw **quickly**.

I draw **happily**.

I draw **beautifully**.

Exercise 2

deeply

restlessly

soundly

I sleep _____.

Exercise 3

I draw **today**.

I draw **early**.

I draw **late**.

Exercise 4

earlier

yesterday

already

I shopped _____.

Exercise 5

I draw **outside**.

I draw **upstairs**.

I draw **everywhere**.

Exercise 6

here

nearby

inside

I study _____.

Exercise 7

I draw **hourly**.

I draw **daily**.

I draw **seldom**.

Exercise 8

daily

sometimes

rarely

I watch television _____.

Exercise 9

1. Sloths move slowly.

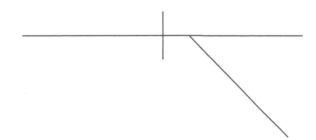

2. I cooked earlier.

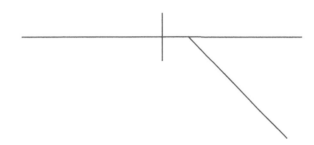

3. Grizzlies hibernate nearby.

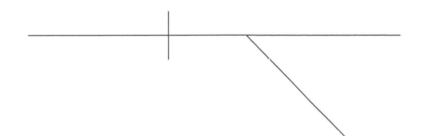

4. Winston Churchill napped daily.

Exercise 10

too

very

really

quite

slightly

Exercise 11

too tired

very tired

really tired

quite tired

slightly tired

Seagulls are too greedy!

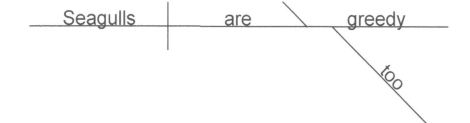

Exercise 12

too late

very late

really late

quite late

slightly late

The bus stopped very quickly.

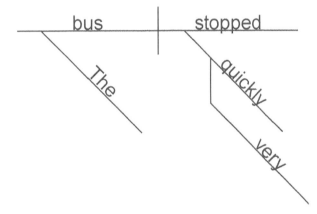

1.   Gifts are very exciting.

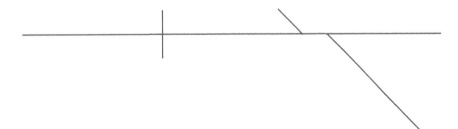

2.   Grandpa was really generous.

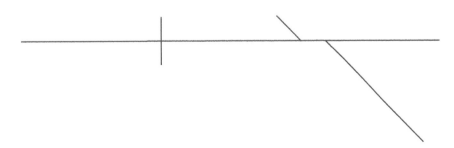

(Exercise 12 continues on the next page.)

3.   Chip wrote really carefully.

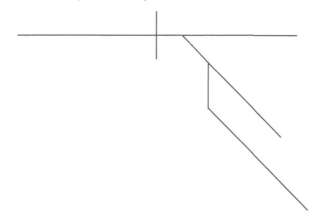

4.   They finished too early.

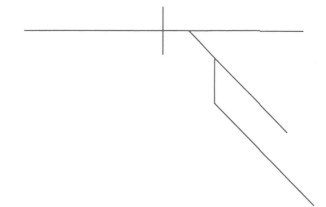

LESSON 81

Exercise 1

1. A volcanic eruption can cause a deadly mudflow.   Statement

2. Evacuate immediately.   Command

3. Should we cross a bridge if we see a mudflow?   Question

4. Mudflows can move faster than you can run!   Exclamation

Exercise 2

S = Statement   C = Command   Q = Question   E = Exclamation

1. Leave the area when a volcano erupts! _____

2. Volcanoes can be very explosive! _____

3. How do volcanoes form? _____

4. Volcanic eruptions can be predicted. _____

5. Make evacuation plans if you live near a volcano. _____

6. Some volcanoes spew lava and rocks high into the air! _____

7. Magma is hot, liquid rock under the earth's surface. _____

8. Did you know that volcanic ash helps make rich soil? _____

Exercise 3

Volcanoes blast lava upward.

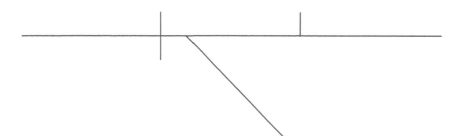

Exercise 4

Leave the dangerous area!

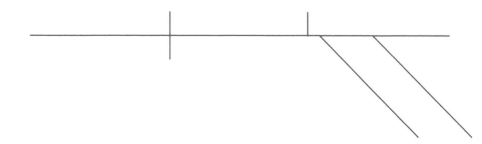

Exercise 5

Can we predict eruptions?

We can predict eruptions.

Exercise 6

India's mudflow was devastating!

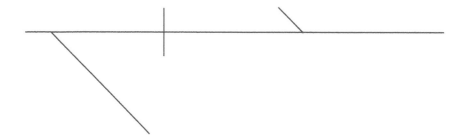

LESSON 82

Exercise 1

dark

fuzzy

sad

active

Exercise 2

this

these

fourth

next

Exercise 3

twenty

most

some

Exercise 4

bee's

student's

Grandpa's

musicians'

Exercise 5

Articles are little words,

You need know only three.

The articles that describe nouns

are **a**, **an**, **the**.

Exercise 6

A jaguar is a large, spotted cat.

The space station is an artificial satellite of Earth.

The moon is a natural satellite.

Exercise 7

old book

older book

oldest book

Exercise 8

● I will sip three soups.

The tomato soup is **creamy**.

The mushroom soup is **creamier**.

The potato and cheese soup is **creamiest**.

I must use up these bananas.

I will eat the **ripe** banana.

I will blend the **riper** banana in my milkshake.

I will mash up the **ripest** banana for banana bread.

Iron is **hard**.

● Steel is **harder**.

Diamonds are **hardest**.

Red stars are **hot**.

White stars are **hotter**.

Blue stars are the **hottest** of all.

●

Exercise 9

1. That horse is dark.

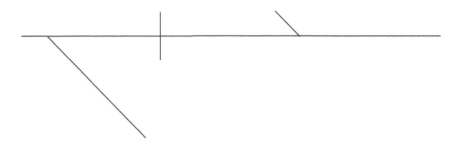

2. A darker horse whinnies.

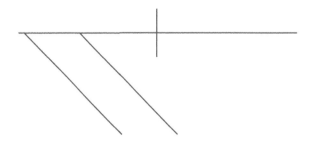

3. The darkest horse gallops.

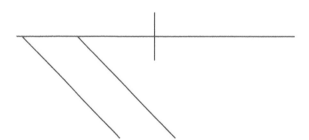

LESSON 83

Exercise 1

Yikes, the bathtub is overflowing!

Wow! That is a giant watermelon!

Ouch! My sunburn is painful.

Exercise 2

Quick

Eek

Great

Oops

Exercise 3

1. Quick! Come here.

_____

2. Good! We won!

_____

3. Oh, I spilt juice.

_____

Exercise 4

Quick! Come here.

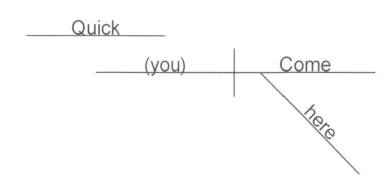

Exercise 5

Good! We won!

Exercise 6

Oh, I spilt juice.

Exercise 7

1. it is _____

2. I would _____

264

3. will not _____

4. can not _____

5. are not _____

6. they will _____

7. I have _____

8. I am _____

9. you are _____

10. we have _____

Exercise 8

1. **We will** go shopping.

    _____

2. **It is** time to go now.

    _____

3. **Let us** eat lunch there.

    _____

4. There **were not** any sales at the stores.

    _____

    _____

5. We **could not** find anything we wanted.

    _____

    _____

LESSON 84

Exercise 1

Pronouns

I, me, my, mine

You, your, yours

He, she, him, her, it

His, hers, its

We, us, our, ours

They, them, their, theirs

Exercise 2

1. The worm wriggles in the dirt.

2. I snuggle next to my mom.

3. The doorbell rang.

4. My rabbit nibbles his food.

5. The squirrel climbs up a tree.

266

Exercise 3

Jets race.

Construction workers operate giant excavators carefully.

workers	operate	excavators
Construction	carefully	giant

Dictation Exercise

Optional Follow-Up

country _____

ocean _____

river _____

city _____

lake _____

mountains _____

Review: Prepositions

Exercise 1

Prepositions

Aboard, about, above, across.

After, against, along, among, around, at.

Before, behind, below, beneath.

Beside, between, beyond, by.

Down, during, except, for, from.

In, inside, into, like.

Near, of, off, on, over.

Past, since, through, throughout.

To, toward, under, underneath.

Until, up, upon.

With, within, without.

Exercise 2

1. The book before me is my grammar book.

2. The shoe under the bed was dusty.

3. The camel in the desert drank water.

Exercise 3

1. The uniform on the conductor is fancy.

2. The sandwich without mustard is mine.

3. The windows throughout the house are open.

4. The player near the referee is injured.

5. I will wear the shirt with the purple stripes.

Exercise 4

I ate the muffin with raisins.

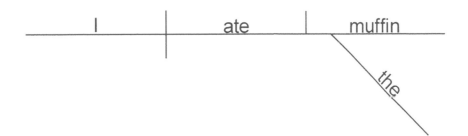

Exercise 5

1. We saw some bugs underneath logs.

2. The weather after the storm was cooler.

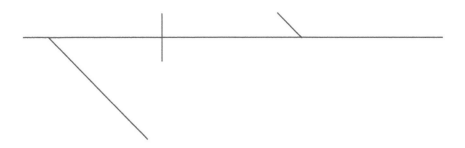

3. The cat with the kittens is gray.

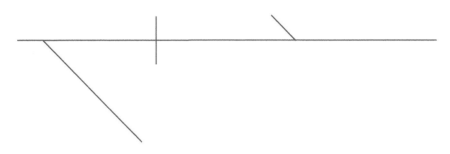

4. Many cars on the freeway sped.

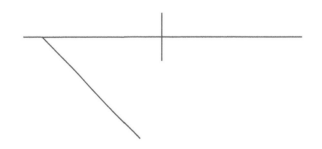

5. Hank found two dimes in the grass.

Exercise 6

●

Inside the bottom drawer of the large wooden desk in the dusty library with the tall shelves of ancient books, Jeremy uncovered a mysterious book with faded gold lettering across its tattered cover.

●

●

LESSON 86

Exercise 1

and

but

or

Exercise 2

<u>Brenna</u> **and** <u>Jenna</u> make necklaces.

Nathan may play <u>football</u> **or** <u>tennis</u>.

<u>Abigail would like to stay up late</u>, **but** <u>it is time to go to bed</u>.

Exercise 3

Jane or Chris can hide.

The wind howls and moans.

Exercise 4

Michael draws.

Vivian paints.

Michael draws, but Vivian paints.

Exercise 5

1. Frogs and bats hibernate.

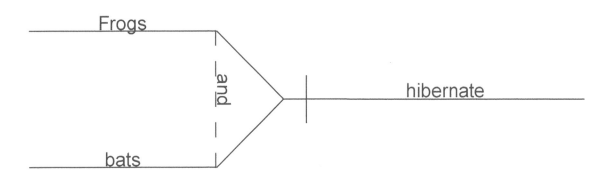

2. Branches sway and bend.

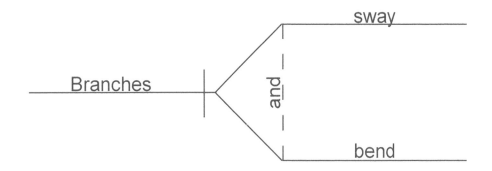

3. Gibbons and marmosets climb and swing.

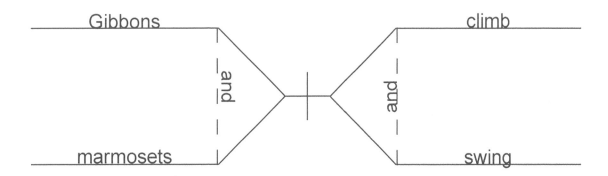

Exercise 6

1.   Dolphins and whales sing and migrate.

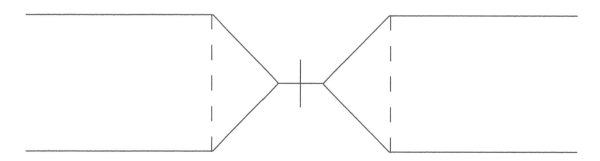

2.   Moths and butterflies flit and flutter.

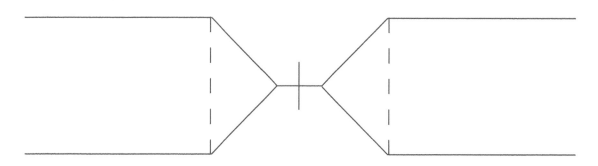

3.   Gulls and pelicans swim and fly.

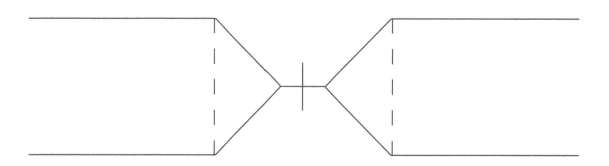

LESSON 87

Exercise 1

1.   I will pack binoculars and a swimsuit.

2.   I will pack binoculars and a swimsuit and pajamas and a toothbrush.

3.   I will pack binoculars, a swimsuit, pajamas, and a toothbrush.

Exercise 2

I am making brownies. I mix flour, sugar, oil, eggs, and chocolate.

I have many collections. I collect stickers, bugs, rocks, coins, and junk.

I went to the aquarium. I saw fish, dolphins, penguins, seals, and stingrays.

(This lesson continues on the next page.)

Exercise 3

1. Solid, liquid, and gas are the three forms of matter.

2. Cars have fenders, tires, engines, and gears.

3. Stormy weather can bring rain, sleet, snow, and wind.

Exercise 4

● **Jordan,** stop teasing your sister.

Patricia, are you aggravating him?

Exercise 5

● Greg asked, **"What is my job today?"**

Dad answered, **"Take out the trash."**

Brad stated, **"I'll pick up, vacuum, and dust."**

Jess exclaimed, **"We'll be through in no time!"**

●

Exercise 6

1. Greg asked, "What is my job today?"

---

2. Dad answered, "Take out the trash."

---

3. Brad stated, "I'll pick up, vacuum, and dust."

---

4. Jess exclaimed, "We'll be through in no time!"

Exercise 7

"**What is my job today?**" Greg asked.

"**Take out the trash,**" Dad said.

"**I'll pick up, vacuum, and dust,**" Brad stated.

"**We'll be through in no time!**" Jess exclaimed.

Exercise 8

1. "What is my job today?" Greg asked.

2. "Take out the trash," Dad said.

3. "I'll pick up, vacuum, and dust," Brad stated.

4. "We'll be through in no time!" Jess exclaimed.

Exercise 9

1. "What is my job today?" Greg asked.

   Greg asked his father what his job was for the day.

2. Dad said, "Take out the trash."

   Dad told Greg to take out the trash.

3. "I'll pick up, vacuum, and dust," Brad stated.

   Brad promised to pick up the books on the floor, vacuum the rug, and dust the table.

4. Jess exclaimed, "We'll be through in no time!"

   Jess exclaimed that she thought they would be finished cleaning in no time.

LESSON 88

Review: Diagramming

Exercise 1

1.   Scrooge scared children.

2.   Mean Scrooge scared children.

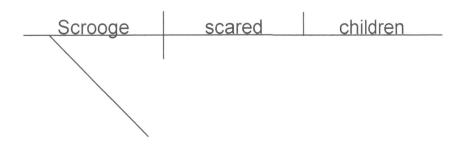

3.   Mean Scrooge scared little children.

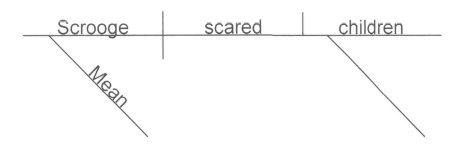

4.   Mean Scrooge scared little children often.

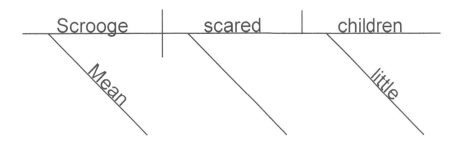

Exercise 2

Bob Cratchit copied numbers.

Diligent Bob Cratchit copied numbers.

Bob Cratchit | copied | numbers

Diligent Bob Cratchit copied Scrooge's numbers.

Bob Cratchit | copied | numbers
Diligent

Diligent Bob Cratchit copied Scrooge's numbers daily.

Bob Cratchit | copied | numbers
Diligent   _Scrooge's_

Exercise 3

Bob Cratchit loved Tiny Tim.

Kind Bob Cratchit loved Tiny Tim.

| Bob Cratchit | loved | Tiny Tim |

Kind Bob Cratchit loved cheerful Tiny Tim.

| Bob Cratchit | loved | Tiny Tim |

Kind

cheerful

Kind Bob Cratchit loved cheerful Tiny Tim dearly.

| Bob Cratchit | loved | Tiny Tim |

Kind

cheerful

Exercise 4

Ghosts visited Scrooge.

Three ghosts visited Scrooge.

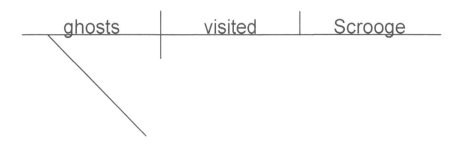

Three ghosts visited stingy Scrooge.

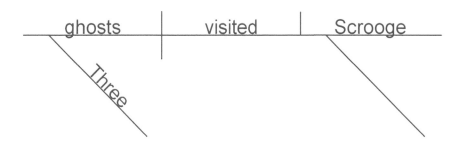

Three ghosts visited stingy Scrooge unexpectedly.

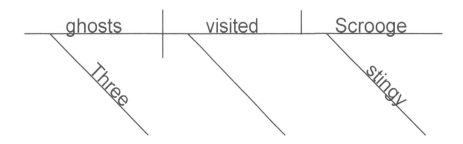

Exercise 5

1. Joseph Lister is a famous doctor.

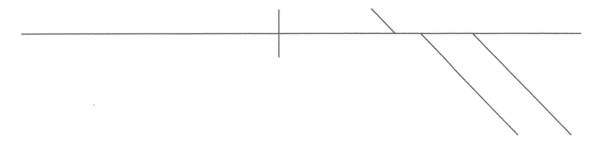

2. Melvil Dewey was an influential librarian.

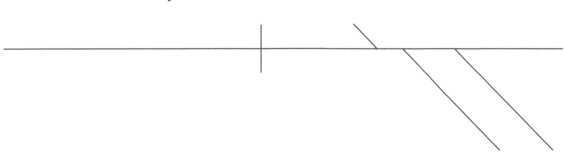

3. King Solomon was very wise.

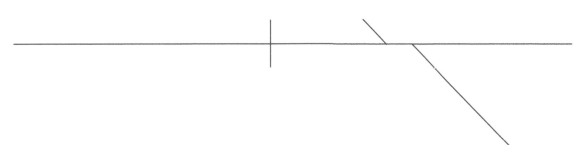

4. Lewis Carroll was quite imaginative.

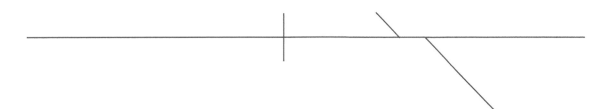

LESSON 89

I have recited the title, the author, and the poem.

☐ "The Land of Nod" by Robert Louis Stevenson

☐ "A Tragic Story" by William Makepeace Thackeray

☐ "I Wandered Lonely As a Cloud" by William Wordsworth

☐ "A Time to Talk" by Robert Frost

☐ "The Bells" by Edgar Allan Poe

☐ "A Slash of Blue" by Emily Dickinson

Writing Dates

Thank-You Letter Rough Draft

Exercise 1

The Months
A Mother Goose Rhyme

Thirty days hath September,

April, June, and November;

All the rest have thirty-one,

Except for February alone,

Which has four and twenty-four

Till leap year gives it one day more.

Exercise 2

1. _____ [Instructor]

   _____ [Student]

2. _____ [Instructor]

   _____ [Student]

3. _____ [Instructor]

   _____ [Student]

4. _____ [Instructor]

   _____ [Student]

Thank-You Letter Rough Draft

_____

_____

<u>Final Thank-You Letter Checklist</u>

Date

- ☐ date is written in upper right-hand corner of page
- ☐ month is capitalized and not abbreviated
- ☐ comma is placed after the day of the month

Greeting

- ☐ "Dear" begins with a capital letter
- ☐ appropriate title of respect is capitalized, abbreviated, and ends with a period
- ☐ person's name begins with a capital letter
- ☐ comma is placed after the person's name

Body of the Letter

- ☐ paragraph is indented
- ☐ each sentence begins with a capital letter
- ☐ each sentence ends with a mark of punctuation

Closing

- ☐ closing is written on the right-hand side of the paper
- ☐ first word in closing is capitalized
- ☐ closing is followed by comma

Writer's Name

- ☐ name is written under closing
- ☐ first letters in the name are capitalized

Addressing the Envelope

Exercise 1

_____

_____

_____

Exercise 2

Name	Abbreviation
Avenue	Ave.
Boulevard	Blvd.
Circle	Cir.
Court	Ct.
Drive	Dr.
Highway	Hwy.
Lane	Ln.
Road	Rd.
Street	St.

Exercise 3

Our state abbreviation is _____.

Exercise 4

_____

_____

_____

Exercise 5

_____

_____

_____

Exercise 6

_____

_____

_____

_____

_____

_____

_____

_____

_____

_____

Friendly Letter Rough Draft

Final Friendly Letter Checklist

Date

- ☐ date is written in upper right-hand corner of page
- ☐ month is capitalized and not abbreviated
- ☐ comma is placed after the day of the month

Greeting

- ☐ "Dear" begins with a capital letter
- ☐ appropriate title of respect is capitalized, abbreviated, and ends with a period
- ☐ person's name begins with a capital letter
- ☐ comma is placed after the person's name

Body of the Letter

- ☐ paragraph is indented
- ☐ each sentence begins with a capital letter
- ☐ each sentence ends with a mark of punctuation

Closing

- ☐ closing is written on the right-hand side of the paper
- ☐ first word in closing is capitalized
- ☐ closing is followed by comma

Writer's Name

- ☐ name is written under closing
- ☐ first letters in the name are capitalized

Who Has Seen the Wind?

by Christina G. Rossetti

Who has seen the wind?

Neither I nor you;

But when the leaves hang trembling

The wind is passing through.

Who has seen the wind?

Neither you nor I;

But when the trees bow down their heads

The wind is passing by.

Copying a Poem Checklist

Title

☐   each word in title is capitalized except for "the"

Author's Name

☐   "by" is not capitalized

☐   name of author is capitalized

☐   initial is capitalized and followed by a period

Body of Poem

☐   first word in each line is capitalized

☐   lines are punctuated exactly like the original poem

☐   there is a space between the two stanzas

DICTIONARY SKILLS LESSON 1

Exercise 1

apple

banana

carrot

Exercise 2

turtle

duck

zebra

Exercise 3

duck

turtle

zebra

Exercise 4

circle   _____

fun   _____

down   _____

(Exercise 4 continues on the next page.)

out   _____

key   _____

man   _____

salt   _____

run   _____

under   _____

sing   _____

hand   _____

bent   _____

zoo   _____

look   _____

ant   _____

Exercise 5

g**o**

g**e**t

g**r**ass

Exercise 6

get

go

grass

Exercise 7

act   _____

away   _____

able   _____

after   _____

add   _____

Exercise 8

get   _____

gold   _____

grow   _____

glass   _____

give   _____

mind   _____

mess   _____

man   _____

mold   _____

much   _____

step   _____

swim   _____

slip   _____

skin   _____

seed   _____

Optional Follow-Up

List 1	List 2	List 3	List 4	List 5
ball	dive	obey	red	this
born	drop	open	race	tag
beat	date	off	ride	ten
bit	down	one	run	torn
blue	dust	old	roll	tip

Alphabetizing by Third Letter

Exercise 1

car   _____

can   _____

cab   _____

cake   _____

cage   _____

fan   _____

fat   _____

fast   _____

face   _____

fall   _____

gas   _____

gap   _____

gang   _____

gain   _____

gate   _____

hat   _____

ham   _____

hard   _____

hand   _____

have   _____

Optional Follow-Up

List 1	List 2	List 3	List 4	List 5
eat	hay	fig	grab	lot
ear	hall	fin	grill	low
each	hair	fish	grow	lost
easy	hawk	five	great	love
eagle	hang	file	grudge	loud

DICTIONARY SKILLS LESSON 3

Exercise 1

A B C D E F G

H I J K L M N O P

Q R S T U V W X Y Z

Exercise 2

chill

arm

Exercise 3

hot

loaf

Exercise 4

shoe

under

DICTIONARY SKILLS LESSON 4

Exercise 1

A B C D E F G

H I J K L M N O P

Q R S T U V W X Y Z

Exercise 2

dormouse

navigate

skeptical

peanut

Exercise 3

1.   When I go to the zoo, I feed each of the enormous elephants a **peanut**. The elephants use their trunks to grab the nuts.

2.   When I go to the zoo, I feed each of the enormous elephants a **pea-nut**. The elephants use their trunks to grab the nuts.

Exercise 4

adj	adjective
adv	adverb
conj	conjunction
interj	interjection
n	noun
prep	preposition
pron	pronoun
vb	verb

Exercise 5

I live in California, but I spend holidays with my grandparents in the **East**.

Exercise 6

sing	singular
pl	plural

Exercise 7

child \child\ *n, pl* **chil•dren**

foot	*pl*	_____
tooth	*pl*	_____
mouse	*pl*	_____
man	*pl*	_____

DICTIONARY SKILLS LESSON 5

Exercise 1

air

plane

base

ball

Exercise 2

airplane

baseball

Exercise 3

brother

teacher

Friday

Thursday

Tuesday

photo

suggest

about

among

again

divide

because

Exercise 4

●

broth-er

teach-er

Fri-day

Thurs-day

Tues-day

pho-to

sug-**gest**

a-**bout**

a-**mong**

a-**gain**

di-**vide**

●

be-**cause**

Exercise 5

so-fa

so-da

lem-on

ex-tra

chi-na

ba-con

●

Exercise 6

among

about

again

upon

lemon

extra

china

divide

DICTIONARY SKILLS LESSON 6

Words with More Than One Meaning and/or Pronunciation

Exercise 1

1. \ak-shən\

2. \skül\

3. \häl-ij\

4. \äp-ə-rāt\

5. \ad-vər-tīz\

6. \ak-sə-dent-l\

Optional Challenge Word

7. \kə-līd-ə-skōp\

Exercise 2

I can pick up my baby sister, because she is so **light**.

My baby sister wants **light** in her room at bedtime.

Exercise 3

adj	adjective
adv	adverb
n	noun
vb	verb

Exercise 4

My favorite shrub in the yard is called a **box**.

Exercise 5

1. The delivery man put a **box** on our porch.

2. Our family eats a **box** of cereal every day.

3. The President and his wife sit in a special **box** at the theater.

Exercise 6

Will you **box** up that cake for me?

Exercise 7

The two men plan to **box** in the ring tonight.

Exercise 8

The girl in the play has a pink **bow** in her hair.

In the play, the father and son **bow** when the girl enters the room.

Exercise 9

1. The soldier received a **wound** in battle.

2. Her ugly words left a **wound** in my heart.

Exercise 10

1. Stepping on glass can **wound** your foot.

2. Gossip can **wound** your reputation.

Exercise 11

He **wound** the kite's string when the wind grew too strong.

Optional Follow-Up

● These are words that are spelled and pronounced alike but have different

meanings.

> pen
>
> bear
>
> rose

These are words that are spelled alike but have different meanings and

different pronunciations.

> object
>
> present

●

●

Exercise 1

I am **afraid** of the dark.

I am **scared** of the dark.

I am **frightened** of the dark.

Exercise 2

At the National Museum of Natural History, I gazed at the skull of the Tyrannosaurus rex. It was **huge**. It was bigger than I was! Inside the jaws were
huge, pointed teeth. I read that one tooth was thirteen inches long. That
is one inch longer than my ruler. The Tyrannosaurus rex needed its **huge**
teeth and powerful jaws. It could crush five hundred pounds of meat and
bone in a single bite. That animal had a **huge** appetite!

Exercise 3

huge

enormous

immense

gigantic

Exercise 4

ANTONYM: tiny

Exercise 5

1. A **tiny** insect landed on my nose.

2. My mother insists that my room always be **neat**.

3. I always bid goodbye to my guests when they **leave**.

4. I love the smell of **new** sneakers.

5. I like my bath water to be very **hot**.

6. After our Thanksgiving feast, my stomach felt so **full**.

Exercise 1

1. Today you **play**.

2. Yesterday you **played**.

3. Tomorrow you **will play**.

Exercise 2

1. Sally **planted** some flowers yesterday.

2. He **will collect** seashells at the beach tomorrow.

3. Last week, the baby **walked** to me.

4. I **smell** cookies baking in the oven.

5. You **shall clean** your room this afternoon.

6. She **chases** butterflies.

Exercise 3

1. Manuel **floats** in the pool.

2. Bobby **winked** at his sister.

3. The kitten **will drink** milk from a saucer.

4. A flock of birds **flew** across the sky.

5. Many bees **buzz** around the flowers.

6. We **shall rest** after the hike.

7. I **laughed** at the joke.

8. The baker **will sell** us bread.

ORAL USAGE LESSON 2

Irregular Verbs

Exercise 1

I **eat** an apple today.

I **ate** an apple yesterday.

I **have eaten** an apple every day this week.

I **do** my school work today.

I **did** my school work yesterday.

I **have done** my school work every day this week.

I **see** the moon today.

I **saw** the moon yesterday.

I **have seen** the moon every day this week.

I **sing** a song today.

I **sang** a song yesterday.

I **have sung** a song every day this week.

I **go** to the library today.

I **went** to the library yesterday.

I **have gone** the library every day this week.

(Exercise 1 continues on the next page.)

I **drink** water today.

I **drank** water yesterday.

I **have drunk** water every day this week.

I **come** home today.

I **came** home yesterday.

I **have come** home every day this week.

I **write** spelling words today.

I **wrote** spelling words yesterday.

I **have written** spelling words every day this week.

Exercise 2

1. That was the sweetest cookie I **have eaten** at this bakery.

2. I already **did** my spelling.

3. I **saw** you at the park yesterday.

4. Last night Mary **sang** a lullaby to the baby.

5. He **has gone** to the store every day.

6. Last Tuesday I **drank** freshly squeezed orange juice with my breakfast.

7. Jin **has come** to play in the pool with us.

8. I **had written** my name on the card before the party.

Irregular Verbs

Exercise 1

I **ring** a bell today.

I **rang** a bell yesterday.

I **have rung** a bell every day this week.

I **draw** pictures today.

I **drew** pictures yesterday.

I **have drawn** pictures every day this week.

I **begin** my daily chores today.

I **began** my daily chores yesterday.

I **have begun** my daily chores every day this week.

I **bring** pencils today.

I **brought** pencils yesterday.

I **have brought** pencils every day this week.

I **run** around the house today.

I **ran** around the house yesterday.

I **have run** around the house every day this week.

I **give** help today.

I **gave** help yesterday.

I **have given** help every day this week.

I **throw** the ball today.

I **threw** the ball yesterday.

I **have thrown** the ball every day this week.

I **think** about summer today.

I **thought** about summer yesterday.

I **have thought** about summer every day this week.

I **wear** a coat today.

I **wore** a coat yesterday.

I **have worn** a coat every day this week.

Exercise 2

1. Last Fourth of July, the bell in the tower **rang** four times.

2. Tommy **drew** a picture and gave it to his mother.

3. The parade **began** at eight o'clock yesterday morning.

4. I **brought** my mother flowers on her last birthday.

5. My brother **has run** a race.

6. I **have given** a cracker to the baby every day.

7. Joe **threw** the ball over the fence last night.

8. I **thought** I had lost this money.

9. He **has worn** out his best pants.

Irregular Verbs: Lay Verus Lie, Set Versus Sit

Exercise 1

1.   I **lay** my head on my pillow.

2.   The mother **is laying** the baby in her crib.

3.   The chicken **laid** a brown egg in the nest.

4.   I **laid** my flashlight on the table last night.

5.   Every past Memorial Day people **have laid** flowers on graves of soldiers.

Exercise 2

1.   I **lie** on my bed.

2.   The book **is lying** on the table beside my bed.

3.   The mouse **lay** in the straw yesterday.

4.   Every clear night I **have lain** on the grass to look at the stars.

Exercise 3

1.   Please pick up the book that **is lying** on the floor.

2.   Now I **lay** me down to sleep.

3.   Jane **lies** on the sofa.

4.   Grandma **is laying** her groceries on the table.

5.   The goose **laid** a golden egg.

6.   Every spring I **have lain** on the hammock and enjoyed the warm weather.

(Exercise 3 continues on the next page.)

7. Yesterday I **laid** my notebook here.

8. Every past Hanukkah my parents **have laid** presents near the menorah.

9. The rabbit **lay** in the straw last night.

Exercise 4

1. **Set** the dishes on the table.

2. Marcus **is setting** the groceries in the pantry.

3. The volunteers **set** extra chairs in the back of the church last Sunday.

4. Every night for the past week I **have set** a book on my bed.

Exercise 5

1. I **sit** at the table for breakfast.

2. My sister **is sitting** with me.

3. We **sat** there yesterday, too.

4. We **have sat** there every morning this week.

Exercise 6

1. I **sat** in the back seat when we went to town.

2. **Set** the laundry baskets on the floor.

3. My babysitter **is sitting** with me.

4. Joseph **is setting** his models on a table.

5. The movers **set** our boxes in the proper rooms last week.

6. You **sit** at the desk.

7. We **have sat** in the bleachers for every game this season.

8. Every day for the past week I **have set** a different toy on the shelf.

Exercise 7

Set a plate on the table.	Sit in a big chair
Set a stuffed animal on the floor.	Make the stuffed animal sit in a chair.
Lay a blanket on the sofa or the bed.	Lie on the sofa or the bed.
Lay your head on your arms.	Make a stuffed animal lie on the bed next to you.

ORAL USAGE LESSON 5

Exercise 1

Subject Pronouns	Object Pronouns
I	me
he	him
she	her
we	us
they	them

Exercise 2

I made some cookies.

He ate the cookies.

She helped him eat the cookies.

We cleaned up the kitchen.

They had a good time.

Fred and **I** rode bikes.

Daphne and **he** made the cookies.

She and Edward built a sandcastle.

We and the rest of the team celebrated the victory.

They and the other neighbors surprised Mary.

Exercise 3

George tickled him.

Exercise 4

Doug helped **me**.

Carol thanks **him**.

The dog followed **her**.

The family welcomes **us**.

Mother forgave **them**.

Charles chased Tom and **me** around the yard.

Aunt Bess took **him** and **me** to the library.

The neighbor paid Lucy and **her** for the lemonade.

Grandpa asked Mom and **us** for a ride.

Max invited **them** and **me** to the party.

Exercise 5

It is I.

It is **he**.

It is **she**.

It is **we**.

It is **they**.

It was I who brought the cake.

It was **he** who ate some cake.

It was **she** who asked for an extra slice.

It was **we** who finished the whole cake.

It was **they** who baked another cake.

Did you think that it was I who won?

It must have been **he** who won.

Was it you and **she** who entered the next race?

Was it **he** and **they** who judged the competition?

Are those the books? Those are **they**.

Was it **he** who lent the books? It was **he**.

Ring! Ring!

    Hello.

May I please speak with Alex?

    This is he.

Was it you who sent the gift?

    It was I.

Ring! Ring!

    Hello.

May I please speak with Lee?

    This is she.

Was it Joe who sprained his ankle?

    It must have been he.

Ring! Ring!

    Hello.

May I please speak with Chip?

    This is he.

Was it Sam and she who won the prizes?

    It was Sam and she.

Irregular Verbs: "To Be"

Exercise 1

I **am** hungry.

Mary and Jen **were** going to the store.

Are you thirsty?

Jimmy's snowballs **are** melting.

I **am** in the car.

She **is** in the car.

You **were** there yesterday.

Ben and I **are** in the third grade.

Roses and daisies **are** flowers.

The boys **were** tired.

I **was** happy.

We **are** going with you.

Were you at the party?

You **are** smart.

Were Sherri and Blake at the store?

My baby sister **was** born in the hospital.

Exercise 2

am

is

are

was

were

Exercise 3

1. Martha is in the kitchen.

2. You were outside.

3. The people were arriving.

4. I was excited.

5. Lois and I are ready.

6. I am dressed up.

7. Joe and Simon were in the yard.

8. Are you going to stay?

9. Terry's cookies are crumbling.

10. I am cleaning up.

11. Were you going to leave?

12. You are helpful.

13. Were Jake and Patsy at the party?

14. A napkin and a cup are on the floor.

15. We are sweeping up the crumbs.

16. My mother was happy.

Exercise 1

no

not

nobody

nowhere

nothing

no one

never

neither

hardly

barely

scarcely

Exercise 2

I'm **not** doing anything.

I'm doing **nothing**.

He **doesn't** want any help.

He wants **no** help.

(Exercise 2 continues on the next page.)

We **won't** ever get there.

We will **never** get there.

I got **hardly** any help.

I **can't** get any help.

I can get **no** help.

I **didn't** get any.

I got **none**.

We **won't** ever cross the street.

We will **never** cross the street.

I **can't** find anybody at home.

I can find **nobody** at home.

I **didn't** go anywhere.

I went **nowhere**.

I **don't** want any more cereal.

I want **no** more cereal.

I **don't** want anybody in my room.

I want **nobody** in my room.

(Exercise 2 continues on the next page.)

Don't get into any trouble.

Get into **no** trouble.

I **didn't** have anything to do.

I had **nothing** to do.

Exercise 3

1.   I could eat a bowl of slimy worms!

      I could **never** eat a bowl of slimy worms!

2.   Everybody loves to get shots.

      Nobody loves to get shots.

3.   I could climb to the top of a skyscraper.

      I could **not** climb to the top of a skyscraper.

4.   A lost ring can be found everywhere.

      A lost ring can be found **nowhere**.

5.   I can easily stand on one foot for five minutes.

      I can **barely** stand on one foot for five minutes.

6.   I did something to cause it to rain.

      I did **nothing** to cause it to rain.

7.   I want chocolate-covered ants for dessert!

      I want **no** chocolate-covered ants for dessert!

I'm **not** going anywhere.

I'm going **nowhere**.

I do **not** have any.

I have **none**.

There was **hardly** anybody on the bus.

There **wasn't** anybody on the bus.

I **wasn't** doing anything.

I was doing **nothing**.

I **don't** get any respect.

I get **no** respect.

I want **none** of those carrots.

I **don't** want any of those carrots.

I **can't** see anyone from my window.

I can see **no one** from my window.

I **didn't** hit anybody.

I hit **nobody**.

The puppy has had **nothing** to eat today.

The puppy has **barely** had anything to eat today.

The team **doesn't** have anybody to cheer for it.

The team has **nobody** to cheer for it.

I **never** ate any of the cookies.

I ate **none** of the cookies.

I **didn't** get enough time to finish.

I **scarcely** got enough time to finish.

Definitions to Be Memorized

A **noun** is the name of a person, place, thing, or idea.

A **pronoun** is a word used in the place of a noun.

A **verb** is a word that does an action, shows a state of being, links two words together, or helps another verb.

An **adjective** is a word that describes a noun or pronoun. Adjectives tell what kind, which one, how many, and whose.

An **adverb** is a word that describes a verb, an adjective, or another adverb. Adverbs tell how, when, where, how often, and to what extent.

A **preposition** is a word that shows the relationship of a noun or pronoun to another word in the sentence.

A **conjunction** is a word that joins words or groups of words together.

An **interjection** is a word that expresses sudden or strong feeling.

A **sentence** is a group of words that expresses a complete thought. All sentences begin with a capital letter and end with a punctuation mark.

Glossary of Additional Terms to Know

command – a sentence that gives an order or makes a request. A command sentence ends with either a period or an exclamation point.

complete predicate – the verb and other words that tell us what is said about the subject. It is the part of the sentence in which the verb is found.

complete subject – the simple subject and other words that tell us who or what the sentence is about. It is the part of the sentence in which the simple subject is found.

compound subject – a subject with two or more parts that are joined by a conjunction.

compound verb – two or more verbs that are joined by a conjunction and that have the same subject.

contraction – two words drawn together and shortened by dropping some letters. Every contraction has an apostrophe in it. The apostrophe tells us where the letters were dropped to form the contraction.

direct object – the noun or pronoun in the complete predicate that receives the action of the verb.

direct quotation – the exact words that someone says. Direct quotations are always enclosed by quotation marks.

exclamation – a sentence that shows sudden or strong feeling. An exclamation always ends with an exclamation point.

homonym – words that are spelled alike and pronounced alike but have different meanings.

indirect quotation – the content of what a person says without using his or her exact words. There are no quotation marks surrounding an indirect quotation.

predicate adjective – an adjective in the complete predicate that describes the subject.

predicate nominative – a noun or pronoun in the complete predicate that renames the subject.

question – a sentence that asks something. A question always ends with a question mark.

simple predicate – the main verb plus any helping verbs.

simple subject – the main word or term that tells us who or what the sentence is about.

statement – a sentence that gives information. Statements always end with a period.

types of sentences – The four different types of sentences are statements, commands, questions, and exclamations.

Summary of Rules

Forming Plurals

- Usually, add **s** to a noun to form the plural.
- Add **es** to nouns ending in **s**, **sh**, **ch**, **x**, or **z**.
- If a noun ends in **y** after a consonant, change the **y** to **i** and add **es**.
- If a noun ends in **y** after a vowel, just add **s**.

Commas in a Series

Put a comma after every item except the last one in the series.

Direct Address

Put a comma after the name or names of the people to whom you are speaking.

Direct Quotation That Comes at the End of a Sentence

- The exact words a person says are always enclosed by quotation marks.
- Direct quotations begin with a capital letter.
- The quotation is separated from the rest of the sentence by a comma.
- The end punctuation mark always comes inside the quotation marks.

Direct Quotation That Comes at the Beginning of a Sentence

- The exact words a person says are always enclosed by quotation marks.
- Direct quotations begin with a capital letter.
- If the direct quotation would normally end with a period, then the period is changed to a comma. This comma is always inside the quotation marks.
- If the direct quotation ends with a question mark or exclamation point, that mark is always inside the quotation marks.
- Since the direct quotation is only a part of the sentence, the larger sentence must have its own end mark.

Lists to Be Memorized

Pronouns

I, me, my, mine

You, your, yours

He, she, him, her, it

His, hers, its

We, us, our, ours

They, them, their, theirs

Helping Verbs

Am

Is

Are, was, were

Be

Being

Been

Have, has, had

Do, does, did

Shall, will, should, would, may, might, must

Can, could

State of Being Verbs

Am

Is

Are, was, were

Be

Being

Been

Linking Verbs

Am

Is

Are, was, were

Be

Being

Been

Prepositions

Aboard, about, above, across.

After, against, along, among, around, at.

Before, behind, below, beneath.

Beside, between, beyond, by.

Down, during, except, for, from.

In, inside, into, like.

Near, of, off, on, over.

Past, since, through, throughout.

To, toward, under, underneath.

Until, up, upon.

With, within, without.

Articles

a, an, the

Common Conjunctions

and, but, or

345